THE JEWISH VALUES SERIES

When a Jew prays

ILLUSTRATIONS BY ERIKA WEIHS

When a Jew prays

by **SEYMOUR ROSSEL**

with Eugene B. Borowitz and Hyman Chanover

THE JEWISH VALUES SERIES

BEHRMAN HOUSE, INC. PUBLISHERS NEW YORK, N.Y.

Dedicated to Chaim and Susan Stern, who lent
their hands to strengthen mine.
And to Jacob—whose dedication
is to children.

WEST ORANGE, N.J.

© *Copyright 1973, by Behrman House, Inc.*

Published by Behrman House, Inc.
235 Watchung Ave., W. Orange, N.J.

Library of Congress Catalog Card Number: 73-1233
Standard Book Number: 87441-093-2

Manufactured in the United States of America
10 9 8 7
DESIGNED BY BETTY BINNS

Acknowledgments

The author and publisher thank the following for permission to reprint:
Central Conference of American Rabbis, *The Union Prayerbook*, New
York: C.C.A.R., 1940; De Sola Pool, David, *The Traditional Prayer Book*,
New York: Behrman House, Inc., 1960; Harlow, Jules, *Maḥzor for Rosh
HaShanah and Yom Kippur*, New York: The Rabbinical Assembly, 1972;
Hertz, Joseph H., *The Authorized Daily Prayer Book*, New York: Bloch
Publishing Co., 1948; Rayner, John D. and Stern, Chaim, ed., *Service
of the Heart*, London: Union of Liberal and Progressive Synagogues,
1967.

Contents

1   *An invitation to prayer*   9

What prayer is

2   *Why people pray*   17
3   *Kavannah*   23
4   *Different kinds of prayer*   33
5   *What prayer does for us*   44
6   *How God answers*   52

The way we pray

7   *Praying together*   63
8   *Prayer and poetry*   74
9   *Giving music to our prayers*   78
10   *The berachah*   88
11   *A formula for mitzvot*   96
12   *Other ways of prayer*   100
13   *A place of prayer*   109

The order of our prayers

14 *Putting it all together*   119

15 *An order of prayer: Step one*   127

16 *An order of prayer: Step two*   136

17 *An order of prayer: Step three*   142

18 *An order of prayer: Step four*   150

19 *Prayer and study*   153

20 *Actions to fit our words*   160

21 *Special services for special times*   164

22 *The closing prayers*   173

Prayer and you

23 *Talking it over*   179

INDEX TO PRAYERS   189
LIST OF LEGENDS AND STORIES   190
INDEX   191

When a Jew prays

The enemies of Daniel came to the king to tell him of all the evil which Daniel had done. When the king asked Daniel to answer, the time for the afternoon prayers had come. So Daniel slipped to his knees (it was his favorite way of praying) and began to recite the Shema.

"What shall be done with one who is guilty and will not answer his king?" asked the enemies.

In this way, Daniel fell to the hands of his enemies. They took him to a den full of lions and threw him to the growling beasts.

It came to pass in the morning, when the enemies returned, Daniel was still alive. All night long he had prayed, and the lions had not eaten him.

Then Daniel's enemies said, "The lions were not hungry."

And the king said, "Let us test and see if they were hungry or not." With that, the king threw all Daniel's enemies into the lions' den. So it was that Daniel's enemies were destroyed by hungry beasts, while Daniel was saved through prayer.

—A legend of Daniel

1

An invitation to prayer

Our people has many legends about prayer.

Throughout the ages, Jews have felt a need to pray. We have found a kind of strength in our prayers. We have tried to bring ourselves closer to God through our prayers; and we have tried to bring our people closer together through prayer and prayer services.

In a way, our prayers are our dreams. Just as you dream at night alone in your bed, the Jewish people has set aside times to dream together. For our prayers bring us visions of a world at peace. Our prayers remind us of what is truly important in the world, of kindness and compassion, of justice and friendship, of life and the world we live in, and of God, who has made us able to dream and to do.

GROWING AND CHANGING
As we grow and change, our
idea of God grows and changes, too.
Jewish prayer and our Jewish
heritage serve to guide us
as we seek to know God better.

But prayers are different from dreams, too. Just what is prayer exactly? What does prayer do? Does prayer really work? Why do we Jews spend so much time praying? What is supposed to happen at a prayer service? Is Jewish prayer different from any other kind of prayer?

Studying prayer

By now you have said many prayers. You have been to Sabbath services. You have prayed. It is only right that you should know what prayer is all about, and what makes prayer special to our people. But it is not easy to answer all the questions that you might have about prayer.

Prayer is very personal. Your prayer always belongs to you. It is your way of speaking with God. While no two people have exactly the same idea of God, Judaism allows each of us to think of God in our own personal way. Therefore, each of us must find his own way to pray, too.

Still, there are things about God and prayer that we do know. After all, the Jewish people has been praying to God for a long, long time. And in all that time, Jews have been seeking the answers to the very same questions that you have today. And we do have some answers, some Jewish answers.

That is why we study about prayer.

Of course, the best way to study about prayer is to **Praying**
pray. The more we pray with our people, the more
we learn about Jewish prayer. And if we pray and
study at the same time, then we can learn a great
deal about what prayer means and how we should
pray.

So although this book will try to help you to learn
about Jewish prayer, it is no substitute for going to
services and praying for yourself. We hope you will
go to services as you study this book. Then you can
think about the ideas in the book while you are praying, and you can think about how it is to pray while
you are studying the ideas of prayer.

This book will try to answer your questions about
prayer. It may answer some questions that you have
not even asked yet. And it may not be able to answer
some of your questions. We do not always know
everything there is to know; it may be up to you
to keep searching, to keep looking for the answers
to some questions.

LEARNING ABOUT PRAYER
The Jewish people has learned much about prayer.
Each of us learns for himself, too. We learn
by studying and by going to prayer services.
We learn through the special feeling that comes
to us as we sing and celebrate together.

A song and a celebration Think of the feeling that you get at services when everyone sings together *En Kelohenu,* "There is none like our God."

אֵין כֵּאלֹהֵינוּ   אֵין כַּאדוֹנֵינוּ
אֵין כְּמַלְכֵּנוּ   אֵין כְּמוֹשִׁיעֵנוּ:

There is none like our God;
There is none like our Lord;
There is none like our King;
There is none like our Savior.

The prayer seems to lift us up; and having everyone sing together makes us feel strong and good. We are all celebrating the same thing. And we are celebrating it together.

Prayer helps us to join together with other people who feel as we do.

Being together We did not come only to celebrate. We came for many other reasons, too. And one of them was to show that we are Jews, and that we are glad to be Jews. The prayers we say and the songs we sing remind us of what it means to be a Jew. They tell about the things that our people believe in, the ideas that have kept the Jewish people alive for so many years.

When we pray together, we thank God for all His mercy and help throughout the ages. We praise God for keeping us one people, even though we are spread out in many places and many lands. In a way, our prayers help to bind us together.

A Jew from Portugal can go to a synagogue where Moroccan Jews are praying and understand their service! A Jew from America can go to a synagogue in Israel and understand the prayer service there!

Prayer helps us in another way, too. It reminds us **Loving our** that our world is precious and unique. Think about **world** how wonderful the fall is, when leaves turn to soft colors and float gently to the ground, decorating our world with beauty.

Or the springtime, when flowers spring suddenly into view, splashing the world with bright reds and yellows, blues and golds. Or think of the sky as the sun is setting, turning to red and orange, a splash of lights on the clouds.

God shows His lovingkindness in every fruit that ripens, in every bud that springs up, in every rain that feeds the earth with water, in every new birth, in every creation.

Because prayer reminds us of how special our world is, it makes us think about how we should behave in the world.

GOD'S LOVINGKINDNESS
We praise God in prayer for His lovingkindness.
We praise Him for bud and blossom and fruit,
for rain and sun. We praise Him for new
life springing around us.

The time to come Prayer reminds us of something else, too. It reminds us that our world can be a better place. There are many problems in our world. There are still things that we need. And there are still new things to learn. We Jews believe that the time will come when all men will turn toward God and follow God's commandments, but we also believe that we must do our part to make that time come.

Our tradition teaches us that in the time to come, a Messiah will lead our people, just as the kings of old led the Israelites. There is a wonderful idea that we Jews have about the coming of the Messiah. We have been taught that the Messiah will come only when we no longer need help. That is, the Messiah will not solve the problems of the world for us. We must do that ourselves. We must change the world and make it better.

We believe that when we pray we help to change the world. Our prayers remind us of what we have to do, and they remind us that God is our partner. God has given us everything that we have through His creation. He has given us laws and commandments in His love for us, and He has given us hope for the time to come.

LOVING AND LOOKING FORWARD
Prayer helps us love God and appreciate
His goodness and the beauty of the
world around us. It helps us to love and obey
God right now. And it helps us look forward
to the time when all men will love God and
keep His commandments.

Can we really give God anything in return? Can our prayer really mean anything to the Creator of all the World, to the King of kings? A Ḥasidic rabbi told this story to explain why God loves the prayer of man:

The nightingale

Once there was a king who loved music very much. In his palace he kept a whole orchestra to entertain him. All day long the musicians would practice and practice, studying new songs and new melodies to delight the king. Then, in the evenings, they would play for the king in his great throne room. Their melodies were as beautiful as the singing of the angels in heaven, and their songs pleased the king. But the king loved music so much that he wanted to hear it always.

Now one of the king's advisers was a wise man, and he brought the king a beautiful songbird, a nightingale. The nightingale sang night and day, flittering from place to place in its golden cage. All day long, no matter what else the king was doing, he would pause to listen to the unpracticed song of the nightingale.

And even though the songbird knew only one melody, the king came to love its singing much more than the playing of his whole orchestra. For the singing of the nightingale came from its heart, from its very soul.

So, too, God, the King of kings, loves the singing of man in prayer much more than all the perfect prayers of the angels, for the prayer of man comes from man's heart. Prayer is truly the "Service of the Heart."

O Lord!
Help me to understand that I am not alone.
When I feel that I am so very small and the world so
very huge,
When I feel that the problems around me are very great
and I am very little,
When I hear of wars that I cannot stop, of hungry people
I cannot feed,
When I see people doing wrong and I cannot help them,
When I hear of people hurting other people,
Help me to remember that You are with me—
Help me to choose You, O Lord, again and again,
To choose the way of life You have taught men to live,
That my world may be just a little better,
Just a little brighter,
Because I was in it.
Amen.

2

Why people pray

There is a first time for everything. The first time you cross the street alone. The first time you go to school. The first time you tie your shoe laces. The first time you sleep over at a friend's house. The first time you go to the synagogue. There are many firsts.

And in the life of the world there are first times, too. The first time the sun shone. The first time a man planted seeds. The first time leaves withered and began to fall. The first time a man used fire. And the first time a man prayed to his God.

We do not know what that first prayer was about. We do not know why man first called out to God. But let's imagine how it might have happened.

Man begins to pray

Once a man stood up straight and looked around him. His eyes were filled with visions. He saw trees whose leaves were green and gold, red and brown. He saw water flowing down toward the sea, its cool blue surface a mirror for the towering sky. He saw fruit ripe on the trees and tasted it. He saw rabbits and field mice, birds and serpents, squirrels and deer. And he thought, "This is a beautiful place." He wondered, "How did all this come to be?" Perhaps he said, "Thanks. Thank You for this wonderful world, You Maker of the World!"

Or perhaps clouds began to fill the sky. The blue heavens disappeared, covered by the dense gray clouds. A chill wind cut through the trees, tearing leaves from the branches and whistling as it passed the man's ears. Then a great rumbling sound broke through the skies and water began to fall from the clouds. It was raining. The man was cold; he was getting wet.

He ran to hide beneath a tree as a sudden bolt of lightning shot from the sky. It lit the air for a moment then cracked with a great roaring sound. When the man turned to look, he saw a great tree split in two and burn to the ground. The rain fell harder and soon it turned into hail which hit the man's head and made him very afraid. The man bent low to the ground. "Save me," he cried out. "Please save me from the rain, from the wind, and the fierce light." Perhaps this was the first prayer.

Or imagine that the rain had stopped. The thunder and the lightning were no more. And the great clouds that had covered the sky broke up into floating cottonlike balls of white fleece. And the bright golden sun warmed the fields and dried them; and warmed the man and dried him, too. Perhaps he said, "What power there is all around me! How good it makes me feel! How great a world this is! May I always be happy in it."

There are other ways in which the first prayer might have been spoken. Perhaps man was very thirsty and could not find a river to drink from. Then he said, "I wish I could find a river." Was he just wishing to himself? Or was he really asking for help? Did he think that the river would somehow answer him? Or did he believe that some power much greater than himself was listening and might really help?

Or imagine that the man was hungry, and as he went searching for food, a wild mountain lion attacked him. The man fought with the lion, but the lion was very strong. Finally the man cried, "Please let me kill this lion." And that may be the way in which the first prayer was spoken. For, often when we say please, we are speaking not to ourselves but to our God.

THE FIRST PRAYER
Who knows what the first prayer was?
A man may pray because he is thankful,
or because he is afraid. He may pray
because he is happy. He may pray because
he needs help. Many "please" prayers are
"help-me" prayers.

We are not alone No matter how the first prayer was spoken, from the earliest times men believed that they were not alone in the world. In the oldest myths and stories, they spoke of gods who looked and acted like people. Some men thought that each field was guarded by a special god who took care of it. Others thought that gods lived on some of the high mountains. Some looked to the sky and said that the sun was a god. Other people believed that the moon was one, too. Whether they found gods in a waterfall or in a stream, in a tree or in an animal, they had a feeling that they were not alone.

They also believed that gods had power, and that while some gods were friendly, some were not. For example, they might have thought that the god of apple trees was a very friendly god who was never angry when you picked his apples but enjoyed giving you presents. But the god of poison ivy was not very friendly. He would make you itch and burn if you just touched his plants. Men tried to use prayer to make friends with their gods.

Men had different feelings about their gods. When they felt the world was too big and hard to understand, they were grateful that their gods were nearby. Perhaps they prayed to thank their gods for staying close to them. When they couldn't understand accidents, sickness, or death, they were afraid of their gods and prayed that the gods would help them and not harm them.

We do not know when or how man began to pray. But we know that wherever there have been men, they have had gods and they have prayed to them.

Although people believed in many gods, they also believed that some gods might be stronger than others. Often just to show that their god was stronger, they would go to war against another tribe or people who had a different god. Believing in many gods almost always meant having many wars.

Many gods mean many wars

Here and there, we find records of people who believed that there was one god more powerful than all the others. Some called this god the Creator and believed that He had made the world. Still, they believed that there were many other less important gods, each with his own special power. They did not yet know that God is One.

The great step forward

When some of these people prayed to their high god, they were praying to God. We know this because the Bible tells us that before the time of Abraham some men called on the name of the Lord. They did not pray to the lesser gods.

One of the first who called on the name of the Lord was Abraham. Abraham saw the people around him sacrificing and praying to many different gods, but he believed that the One God had created the heavens

The One God

ONE GOD, ONE WORLD
Since Abraham's time, we Jews
have understood that there is only One God.
When people believe in many gods, they tend
to make wars. When we pray to One God,
we seek to live in peace with all men.

One GOD
ONE WORLD

and the earth. And that led him to an even more wonderful thought: All people are members of one big family, all created by the One God, the Only God.

Of course, Abraham did not know all of this right away. But he knew that there was only the One God. So he taught this idea to his son Isaac; and made Isaac promise to teach it to his sons and daughters after him. This was the beginning of the Jewish people.

As each generation of the Jewish people learned this truth and lived by it, they saw how much it had to teach them. They began to realize that the One God loved everyone and saw how much better the world could be if they loved everyone, too.

Abraham's sense of the One God meant that people should work for a world free of war. It is not easy to know exactly what to do to bring the world closer to peace; for as long as we remember, people have been making war. But before Abraham, people blamed their wars upon their gods. Now we know that it is not God who makes wars, but people. It is up to us to stop warring and fighting, it is up to us to bring peace into the world. Praying to the One God means dedicating ourselves to peace-bringing.

3

Kavannah

Once two Polish noblemen were drinking and bragging. Each believed that his property was more beautiful and wonderful than the property of the other. The first nobleman said, "I have purchased for a great sum of gold, a fabulous white stallion, the most elegant horse in all the world."

"But of what use is a stallion?" asked the second.

"Why, I can ride him as the clouds ride the wind," said the first.

"That may be," said the other, "but can your stallion give you wisdom?"

"No," answered the first, rubbing his chin.

"Yet there is a man in my court," said the second, "who is one of the world's great teachers. He can teach anything to anyone."

"But can you ride him?" asked the first nobleman, laughing loudly.

"How much better to have a wise adviser, and a great teacher, than a white horse," said the other.

"I will bet that your teacher is not so great as you say."

"What do you mean?" asked the second nobleman.

"Can your teacher teach my horse to pray?"

The second nobleman paused for a minute, but the wine had already reached his head and he could not think clearly. "Of course," he replied.

"If your man can teach my horse to pray in three weeks," said the first, "then the horse is yours. But if he cannot, then you must pay me in gold."

"Agreed," said the second.

But the next morning when the second nobleman woke up and remembered the bet he had made, he was very sad. Horses can trot, they can gallop and canter; but how can a horse pray? Still, the bet had been made. So he called the teacher, whose name was Yussef, to come to him.

"Can you teach a horse to pray?" he asked Yussef, and then he told him of his wager.

When Yussef heard the story from beginning to end, he shook his head. "I do not know," he said. "It seems an impossible task. But I will do my best."

All morning, Yussef did not feed the white stallion and when afternoon came, the beast was very hungry.

Late in the afternoon, Yussef brought out a wooden stand and placed a prayerbook on it. Now he opened the prayerbook to the very first page and spread some oats upon the page.

When the horse smelled the oats, he came over to the prayerbook and ate them from the page where Yussef had placed them.

The next day, Yussef again spread oats on the first page of the prayerbook, but this time he put oats between the next two pages as well. When the horse had eaten all the oats on the first page, he could still smell that there were more oats.

The horse sniffed and sniffed, and finally he put his tongue out and licked the top page, and . . . the page turned. Now the beast ate all the oats that Yussef had placed on the second page.

The next day, Yussef put oats on the first page, on the second page, on the third, and on the fourth page. And whenever the horse finished eating the oats on one page, he put out his tongue and flipped to the next page full of oats.

Soon the time of the wager was up and the two Polish noblemen met again to see who had won the bet. Yussef led the white stallion into the room and set up the stand, placing the prayerbook on top of it. Now of course, there were no oats on the prayerbook pages, but the smell of oats remained on every page.

The horse came up to the prayerbook and sniffed up and down the first page, but finding no oats to eat, he turned the page with his tongue and ran his nose up and down the second page. Soon he had turned through the whole prayerbook, sniffing up and down each page; snorting, grunting, and flipping the pages with his tongue and looking for all the world as if he were praying.

"You see," said the second nobleman to his unfortunate friend, "my little teacher has taught your horse to pray. And so the horse is mine."

Kavannah The horse did not really pray, did he? He looked as if he were praying, but horses cannot pray, can they? Yet how many times do we try to pray as if we were looking for oats in our prayerbook? Or worse. Sometimes we understand the words we say, but we do not think about them.

Here is a prayer that we say before the Shema. Try to think about it as if you were seeing it for the first time. Say it aloud to see if it has a good sound and if you can understand it while you are speaking it.

Lord our God, You have shown us great love and unfailing mercy. Our fathers trusted in You, and You taught them the laws of life. May we trust in You, and learn to understand and love Your Torah.

Let our eyes shine with joy when we study Your Torah; teach us to obey Your commandments, and unite our hearts in the love of Your name.

We praise You, O Lord, who in love have called Your people Israel to serve You.

What does the prayer say? God has shown us His love by giving us laws to follow and we hope that we can *like* following God's laws. If a bully tells you, "You have to do what I tell you to do," then you do not like following his rules. But when someone you love asks you to do something, the task becomes light and easy. Sometimes we even do unpleasant chores because we were asked to do them in a nice way by someone we love.

The author of this prayer was saying that God loves us so much that He gives us His laws to live by. Then he asks a question. Do *you* love God enough to follow those laws every day? Do you love God enough to serve Him?

And there are even more ideas than that in this little prayer. There is a wish that God help us to find joy when we study His laws; a wish that God help to teach us by giving us inspiration; and a hope that some day all men will live together by the same laws, the laws of God.

REJOICING IN THE TORAH
God gave us His wise and good laws
because He loves us. We enjoy learning
His laws, and obeying them; because we,
in turn, love God.

A horse cannot understand these words or see in them these ideas. A horse cannot make these words his own personal prayer and speak them to God. A horse cannot have *kavannah*.

Kavannah is like a feeling. It is what you do inside yourself to make your prayers real. Because it is so personal, and because each of us is different, it is hard to put the feeling of kavannah into words. Like most of our feelings, kavannah is best explained by a story.

Such a story is told about a cantor whose name was Ḥayyim and whose voice was like the clear, round sound of a rosewood flute. When Ḥayyim sang the prayers, the congregation felt the words come to life. And when he chanted a blessing, he put so much feeling into it that the words seemed to rise right up into the heavens.

It happened once, on the morning of Shabbat, as Ḥayyim held the Torah scroll in his arms, carrying it through the congregation and singing, that his voice rose ever more sweetly and the words came out filled with meaning for each person in the congregation.

Up in heaven, the story tells, God was listening to the singing of the Jewish people scattered around the world. And as He listened, one voice came through the rest, a voice filled with such love and sincerity that every word it sang echoed in the

**We Jews have legends of men
so close to God in spirit that they
were said to have walked in heaven.
What do you think it really means
to walk in heaven?**

heavens. "What voice is this that rings so truly?" asked God of his angels.

"It is the voice of Ḥayyim the Cantor, who sings each prayer with all his heart, with all his soul and with all his might," came the reply.

Ḥayyim, far below, was concentrating so hard on what he was singing that when he lifted the Torah scroll above his head, it felt like no weight at all.

Suddenly, the Torah began to rise and Ḥayyim with it. His feet were off the floor and he was rising ever faster, yet the scroll would not let him loose. Instead it carried him out the window and up into the sky.

Finally, Ḥayyim stood before the heavenly throne and he heard the voice of the Lord. "Ḥayyim," the voice said, "tell now the secret of your wondrous prayers. How is it that your words have the power to reach My very throne?"

"When I sing a prayer, I see the words before my eyes, I feel the words forming in my throat, I hear the words ring in my ears, I taste the words in my mouth, and I try with all my heart to understand them," Ḥayyim said.

And the voice of the Lord said, "That is true kavannah. It has lifted you and your prayers to the heavens."

When Ḥayyim returned to his congregation, the people asked where he had been. He answered in the words of the Bible, "The Lord is near to all who call upon Him, to all who call upon Him in truth." And the cantor's eyes shone with joy.

You may say, "But Ḥayyim was a cantor. He had studied how to pray. No wonder he had kavannah." But our rabbis did not think that you had to spend years learning to get kavannah. Anyone could have it, even a person who had never studied at all. The Ḥasidim tell this story:

A simple man came to the synagogue once. During most of the service, he just sat and listened, for he did not know very much. He could not even read the Hebrew of the prayerbook.

All around him the members of the congregation were standing in prayer, each man speaking with God in a whisper. And the simple man wished to speak with God, too. He wished to tell God what a magnificent world He had made. He wished to thank the

Lord for the blessings of health and life. But he could not find the right words to say.

When he thought his heart would break from shame and sadness, he said, "O God, I cannot speak a beautiful prayer for You because I am a simple man and I have forgotten what I studied. I am not good with words. But You, O Lord, You know how to do everything. So I will give You the Alef Bet and You can make a beautiful prayer for Yourself." Then he recited, "Alef . . . Bet . . . Gimel . . . Dalet . . ."

And the rabbi who told this story added, "Of all the prayers spoken that day, this one was the dearest to God."

Kavannah is . . .

Kavannah is the *way* you mean something.

Kavannah is putting your whole heart into each word of a prayer.

Kavannah is saying the words of the prayerbook and thinking about them as if they were your own.

Kavannah is meeting every word you see for the first time, even when you have seen it a hundred times before.

Kavannah is trying to please God through your prayers.

Kavannah is speaking to God in your own special way: by singing, laughing, dancing, or whispering.

Kavannah is feeling the mood of the people you are praying with: the people who sit next to you in the synagogue, the whole congregation that is praying together, the Jewish people who are praying at the same time all around the world, and all people who pray everywhere.

Kavannah is turning words into prayers.

WORDS INTO PRAYERS
What makes words into prayers?
Understanding? Inspiration?
Seeing the words as fresh and new?
What makes words into prayers for you?

4

Different kinds of prayer

Once a boy who had just eaten lunch turned to his mother and said, "Thank you very much." But his mother said, "You should not thank me alone, for I only prepared the food."

The boy wondered, "Whom should I thank?" He went to the grocery store and saw the grocer. "Thank you, Mr. Grocer, for the very fine bread that I ate at lunchtime."

"Oh," said the grocer, "you should not thank me alone. I only sell the bread. I do not bake it."

So the boy went to the bakery where all the bread was made; and there he saw the baker. "Mr. Baker," the boy said, "I want to thank you for the wonderful bread that you bake."

The baker laughed and said, "I bake the bread, but it is good because the flour is good. And the

flour comes from the miller who grinds it."

"Then I will thank the miller," said the boy and he turned to leave.

"But the miller only grinds the wheat," the baker said. "It is the farmer who grows the grain which makes the bread so good."

So the boy went off in search of the farmer. He walked until he came to the edge of the village and there he saw the farmer at work in the fields. "I want to thank you for the bread that I eat every day."

But the farmer said, "Do not thank me alone. I only plant the seed, tend the field, and harvest the grain. It is sunshine and good rain and the rich earth that make the wheat so good."

"But who is left to thank?" asked the boy, and he was very sad, very tired, and very hungry again, for he had walked a long way in one day.

The farmer said, "Come inside and eat with my family and then you will feel better."

So the boy went into the farmhouse with the farmer and sat down to eat with the farmer's family. Each person took a piece of bread and then, all together, they said,

בָּרוּךְ אַתָּה יְיָ. אֱלֹהֵינוּ מֶלֶךְ הָעוֹלָם.
הַמּוֹצִיא לֶחֶם מִן־הָאָרֶץ:

We thank You, O Lord, our God, King of the universe, who bring bread out of the earth.

And then the boy discovered that it was God whom he had forgotten to thank.

We thank You, O Lord...

One of the most important reasons we have for praying as Jews is to thank God for His wonderful gifts. Rabbi Eleazar taught us to "Give to God what is His, for you and all you have are His." When we thank God, we are giving in return.

Giving in return

Imagine that you came walking home from school to see your sister's bicycle lying in the driveway. She must have forgotten to put it away, you said to yourself. So you picked it up, and wheeled it into the garage where it belonged. But your sister did not even notice! All evening long you waited for her to say something, but she had not a word for you.

We forget sometimes to look around us at all the answers God has given to prayers we never spoke. We did not pray for the greatest gift of all, life, and yet it was given to us. We did not pray for health, and yet it was given to us. We did not pray for love, and yet it is given to us. We did not pray for the sunshine, the moonlight, the flowers, the trees, the shimmering stars, or the towering heavens, and yet they were all given to us.

Prayers of thanks always work. When we say thank you for the good things that God has given us, we feel good inside: We know that we have done the right thing, the thing that God would want us to do.

THANK YOU!
We thank each other for good things.
First of all we thank God, who gives us life
and all things good. Our thanks are pleasing
to God. And they add to our happiness, too.

Asking forgiveness

There are times when we do something wrong, too. Sometimes we can hide it from other people, but we can never hide it from God. Doing wrong makes us feel bad. We carry a wrong thing with us like a sack of heavy stones until finally we can say to our mother, our father, our teacher or a friend, "I'm sorry. Forgive me for what I have done."

Often when we do something wrong, we do not mean to. The Hebrew word for sin that we use most, the word *het*, suggests that we have "missed the mark." (It is used, too, when an arrow misses the bull's-eye.) The good things that we do make our lives richer, but when we sin we just miss out on the real rewards of life. Or to be more exact, we usually end up feeling bad about what we have done; that mysterious part of us that seeks to do good is unhappy.

חֵטְא

When we have sinned, we need to come to God and say, "Take this heavy feeling from me—forgive me for what I have done." And one of Judaism's most beautiful beliefs is that, if we ask sincerely, God will forgive us. Indeed, some rabbis taught that God thinks that nothing is better than turning away from sin to do good.

A story is told of an angel who had angered the Lord. When the angel came before the Lord, God said to him, "I will not punish you for your sin, but you must do something to prove you know what I really want."

God then sent the angel to find the *most precious thing* on earth. For many days the angel searched, but he could find nothing that could be called the most precious thing. But one day, on a battleground, the angel found a soldier dying. Then he came to God saying, "Here is the most precious thing. It is the last drop of blood from a man who died to save his country from a tyrant."

"That is very precious," said the Lord, "for that soldier died that others might live a free life. But it is not the *most* precious thing on earth."

So the angel returned to earth and searched again. By chance, he saw a nurse who had worked hard to save the lives of many children. But now, exhausted from her work, she was dying of a fever. The angel took the last breath of the trembling nurse and brought it to God.

When God saw the breath, he said, "That is indeed a very wonderful thing; but even the dying breath of a woman who gave her whole life for others is not the *most* precious thing to me."

The angel returned to earth. And as he wandered from one city to the next, he passed through a deep woods and saw a man on horseback riding.

"Where are you going?" asked the angel.

"I am going to kill a man," said the rider. "He cheated me badly when he sold me a farm and now I am going to kill him." The rider was very angry. He pulled on his horse's reins and rode on.

The angel followed the horse and rider through the woods and soon they came to a small house at the edge of town.

The rider took a gun from his holster and crept up to a window of the small house. The angel followed close behind. Through the window the two watched as the man kissed his children goodnight and put them to bed, tucking the covers under their chins. Suddenly the rider thought of his own family and tears sprang to his eyes.

He put the gun back into its holster and cried, "O Lord, forgive me for what I almost did."

Now the angel understood what was the most precious thing in the world. He took one of the rider's tears and brought it to God.

"Yes," God said, "that is the *most precious thing* to me. To turn away from the wrong and choose instead to do the good, that is the most important thing a man can do. And this tear, which shows that

right or wrong
just or unjust
right or left
free or imprisoned
peace or war...

CHOOSING
God's laws tell us what is right and what is wrong. But God wants us to choose to do right.

he meant it, is the most precious thing on earth. I forgive the man. And now, I forgive you, too, my angel."

Our rabbis teach us that prayers for forgiveness, like prayers of thanks, are always answered. The Medzibozer rebbe said, "We are taught that 'the gates of tears are not closed,' that is, that tearful pleas to God for mercy are accepted by Him."

In class our teacher gives us an assignment to be done at home. We make a note of it in our notebook to remind us. The note helps us to remember what exactly we are supposed to do.

Reminding ourselves

Some of our prayers are "notes to ourselves." They help us to remember why we are praying, what we are praying for, and what we can do to turn our prayers into actions. These are study prayers and in Judaism study is an important form of prayer.

For example, the Shema and the paragraphs following it, are taken from the Bible. When we say the Shema we are really studying the Bible. The Shema and other study prayers talk to us. By praying them, we remind ourselves of what it means to be a good Jew. And because we are saying these words during our prayers to God, we learn that they are very serious.

In the first psalm, there is a line that says, "He studies His Torah day and night." A famous rabbi once asked, "How can a man study both day and night?" Then he answered his own question, saying, "By the reading of Shema." For praying the Shema is studying, too!

Letting go When God saved Moses and the Israelites from the Egyptian chariots at the Red Sea, the Israelites burst into song. Moses' sister, Miriam, "took a tambourine in her hand, and all the women went out after her in dance with tambourines."

Most of our prayer is a kind of celebration. We are celebrating the wonderful world that God has created for us. We are celebrating the gifts that God has given us. And words are not always enough. Sometimes it helps to sing and to dance. Almost all of our prayers have been set to many different melodies, and song is a regular part of almost all prayer services.

In Jerusalem, on the holiday of Simḥat Torah, whole congregations dance out into the streets holding the Torah scrolls high above their heads. And in many Ḥasidic synagogues, dancing around the *Bimah* or "platform" (which is in the center) is a regular part of every service.

NOTEBOOKS AND DANCES
Some prayers are like reminders,
the "notebooks of the mind."
Other prayers call for music,
for song, and dancing, and joy.
Both kinds of prayers are good.

The rabbis called prayer the "service of the heart." **In the**
Words cannot always express what we feel deep down **stillness**
inside. Often we cannot find the right words to speak
to God. And instead we offer our silence.

In everyday life we all tell lies to one another.
Sometimes we don't mean to, but we do anyhow
because we do not tell the whole truth. Other times
we stand by when someone else tells a story that
we know is untrue, but we do not say anything.
That too is a kind of lying. But when we pray, we
cannot tell a lie. God knows our prayer even before
we speak it, for He knows our thoughts. In a way,
He is a part of us, deep inside.

Of course, the most usual kind of prayer is a prayer **Asking for**
that asks God for something. It is not bad to pray **what we**
to God for something that we want, but it is important **need**
to want the right kind of things. The kinds of things
we want tell a lot about the kind of person that we
are.

The person who prays only for things for himself (a new baseball mitt, an embroidery kit, or a new Monopoly set) is praying selfishly. It is better to pray for good for someone else who is in need of it. Rab taught, "If one can pray for the good of his neighbor and does not do so, he is called a sinner."

It is not bad to ask God for the things we need. One of our greatest teachers, Hillel, said, "If I am not for myself, who will be for me?" And it is good to remember that God loves us as much as He loves our neighbors. But Hillel added to his saying, "If I am only for myself, what am I?"

When we pray to ask for things, we show the kind of person that we are. More than that, we also show the kind of God that we believe in. Praying for a piece of bubble gum is like saying magic words to make a ball appear between your fingers. It shows that we think God is nothing more than a magician. But, of course, Judaism teaches us that God is not that at all. Judaism teaches us that God is the source of all, He is the One from which all things come.

A prince was once kidnaped by a roving band of gypsies. The king sent all his armies out to find the lost prince, his only son, but the armies came home empty-handed. Finally, in desperation, the king sent messengers to every corner of his kingdom offering a great reward of silver and gold for the return of his child.

Many years passed before the gypsies returned to the king's land. But when they did, they heard of the reward and hastened to the castle with the prince. The boy had grown older and was dressed all in rags from head to toe. Still the king recognized his son. But the boy had long since forgotten his father and the castle. His eyes bulged when he saw the golden throne and the velvet draperies.

"My son," the father said, "It is so good to have you home again. You may have any gift you choose, anything in the whole wide world is yours for the asking. Fine palaces are yours, jewels and gold are yours. What would you like to have?"

The boy thought for a minute, and then in a small voice, he said, "Could I please have a new pair of shoes?"

Rabbi Simḥa Bunam, who told this story, added a few more words at the end. We are all like the prince when we stand before God, our King. Instead of asking for the wondrous things that God could give us, we forget how wonderful we really are, and so we spend our time asking for the lesser things which have grown to seem very big to us.

Rabbi Eleazar summed up this idea in one sentence. "And when you pray, know before whom you stand." What do we truly need from the Lord of all, the Creator of Heaven and Earth? Rabbi Judah Ha-Ḥasid taught us: "In time of war, the prayer should not be for victory of one side over the other, but it should be for peace—that the Holy One, blessed be He, turn men's hearts to peace."

5

What prayer does for us

We Jews believe that prayer "works." If prayer did not work, we would not pray—it is foolish to do something that makes no sense.

There are two ways to think about how prayer works. One is to see how prayer works on people, on us, how it changes us. The other way is to talk about how our prayers might affect God. It is always much easier to talk about ourselves than to talk about God, so let's begin by asking, "What can prayer do for us?"

Prayer works We spend our lives doing things.

Each morning you get up, wash your face, comb your hair, brush your teeth, eat your breakfast, walk the same path, ride in the same car, go to the same

44

school, see the same people, talk about the same kinds of things, play the same games, come home at the same time, go to sleep and then wake up the next morning to begin all over again. But once in a while, something special happens.

Once in a while, you go to sleep over at a friend's house and wake up in a strange place and do things a little differently. That is special. If you did that every day, it would not be special; it would be ordinary.

When things are special we see them differently. At your friend's house things are much the same as at your own. There is a bed, a sheet, a blanket, a pillow, but because they are different you feel them in a special way. Your friend may have the same toothpaste you have and eat the same cereal for breakfast you do. But in someone else's house they taste different. Even going to school with your friend seems somehow new. And when things are new we can often appreciate them more. That is why we like it when things are special.

If you meet a new friend, that is special. If you stay up late, that is special. If it is Thanksgiving or Pesah, everyone feels that it is special.

Now we are close to seeing one of the most important ways in which prayer works for us. It makes ordinary things special. Let's give an example.

Every Jew feels something special about the Holy Days of Passover. There is all the hustle and bustle of getting ready. There is the wondrous smell of foods being prepared, cakes being baked; the table is being set in a special way. Then there is the meal itself,

the Pesaḥ Seder. But really what makes this meal different from any other?

Surely it is the story that we tell to answer the Four Questions. It is the series of prayers that we say to remind us of what happened on Passover so long ago and how we should feel about it today. It is the sitting together around the table singing the final prayer after the meal. How special that is! How much we enjoy it!

But why wait? Within the Jewish tradition, there is a way to make every meal a special event. Just as we can begin each meal with the blessing of *ha-Motzi*, so too we can end each meal with the singing of *Birkat ha-Mazon*, the Grace after Meals.

בָּרוּךְ אַתָּה יְיָ. אֱלֹהֵינוּ מֶלֶךְ הָעוֹלָם. הַזָּן אֶת־הָעוֹלָם כֻּלּוֹ
בְּטוּבוֹ. בְּחֵן. בְּחֶסֶד. וּבְרַחֲמִים. הוּא נֹתֵן לֶחֶם לְכָל־בָּשָׂר.
כִּי לְעוֹלָם חַסְדּוֹ: וּבְטוּבוֹ הַגָּדוֹל תָּמִיד לֹא־חָסַר לָנוּ.
וְאַל־יֶחְסַר־לָנוּ מָזוֹן לְעוֹלָם וָעֶד: בַּעֲבוּר שְׁמוֹ הַגָּדוֹל:
כִּי הוּא אֵל זָן וּמְפַרְנֵס לַכֹּל. וּמֵטִיב לַכֹּל. וּמֵכִין מָזוֹן
לְכָל־בְּרִיּוֹתָיו אֲשֶׁר בָּרָא. בָּרוּךְ אַתָּה יְיָ. הַזָּן אֶת־הַכֹּל:

We praise You,
O Lord our God,
King of the universe,
Your goodness supports all the world.
With grace,
With love, and with compassion
You provide food enough for all;
Your lovingkindness is everlasting.

Because of Your great goodness,
We do not want;
May we never lack our daily bread.

For You feed and nourish all;
You are good to all,
And You provide food for all Your creatures.

We praise You,
O Lord,
Provider for all.

Saying the Birkat ha-Mazon after each meal makes each meal a celebration. It reminds us that God and man share the task of feeding the world. God provides enough food for all, but we must make sure that all people get enough food. If man can live up to his part of the bargain, then the world will be much closer to peace for all. Many wars are fought because people are hungry and others will not feed them—even though they have more than enough food!

We Jews try to remember that it is our duty to help feed others. In many traditional homes, Jews keep bread on the table at all times so that all who enter, rich or poor, may eat.

BLESSING AND SHARING
"To love is to give." When we
share the bread God gives us,
we acknowledge His love.
We show that we know
God loves us—and that he expects
us to show love for one another.

So you see, we try to make *every* meal special. How does it work? Remember the story of the boy who learned to thank God as well as people? The next time that boy sat down to eat and said ha-Motzi, his meal became something special. Instead of just gulping it down (as a white stallion might eat oats!), he first said a prayer and then, for a minute, his sandwich stood for mother and grocer and baker and farmer and God all working together.

When we Jews drink wine, we say a prayer which reminds us that God himself had a share in creating what we are about to drink.

> *We praise You, O Lord our God, King of the universe, Creator of the fruit of the vine.*

When we Jews eat fruit, we say a prayer which reminds us that God took part in growing the fruit for us to eat.

> *We praise You, O Lord our God, King of the universe, Creator of the fruit of trees.*

Making things special   Of course, it is much easier to make things ordinary. We can gulp down the milk and not think much of it, or say, "It is just milk." We can eat meat without giving it a thought, or say, "It's just something to eat." Saying a prayer reminds us that these things are not ordinary, they are wondrous gifts God has provided through the miracle of His creation.

All things can become special through prayer. When trees seem ordinary, we often forget how beautiful they really are. To help us remember, there is a Jewish prayer just for trees:

We praise You, O Lord our God, King of the Universe, whose world lacks nothing, who have made in it good creatures and goodly trees to give delight to every human being.

The prayer for trees was written by Rabbi Judah the Prince. He wanted Jews to say it when the first blossoms of spring appear on the trees. What a special time! When new life begins.

CELEBRATING LIFE
We celebrate the goodness of God
when we give thanks for each meal,
for wine, for fruit, for trees,
for blossoms.

There is even a Jewish blessing to be said when we see a strange-looking person:

> *We praise You, O Lord our God, King of the Universe,*
> *who give changing forms to your creatures.*

When we say that prayer it reminds us that even strange-looking people are a part of our family. Praying this way, we remember that such people are not freaks, but real, sensitive human beings just like us. We are all children of One God.

Prayer makes us think. It turns the ordinary into the special.

Our special world

What a wonderful world we live in! Everything in it is special to God and can be special to us. Every second is a different second; every minute a different minute; each one happens only once and then never again. We, too, happen only once. You are the one and only you that ever was or ever will be. No one else can ever be you and you can be no one else. You are special.

Praying reminds us just how special we and our world are. It keeps us from forgetting how marvelous our world is and can be.

When something is special to God, we say that it is holy or sacred. And because the whole world is holy to God, we must try to discover the holiness in it. That is what we are saying when we pray:

קָדוֹשׁ. קָדוֹשׁ. קָדוֹשׁ. יְיָ צְבָאוֹת.
מְלֹא כָל־הָאָרֶץ כְּבוֹדוֹ:

> *Holy! Holy! Holy! is the Lord of Hosts;*
> *His glory fills the whole earth.*

Prayer makes the ordinary into the holy, because it helps us to see God's part in all things. We have said, earlier, that prayer is not magic, but now we can see that in truth there is no magic so great as prayer to change the way we see our whole world.

Bringing peace into our world

When we understand that everything is holy to God, then we do not want to do anything to hurt others. We want instead to treasure them, to learn to love them; to live beside them in peace. Without prayer we forget too easily how precious each of God's creatures really is.

Prayer keeps the lessons of Judaism clear before our eyes. It reminds us of the dreams of our prophets and teachers for the time to come when men will turn their weapons into tools and build together a better world.

The famous Zionist, Theodor Herzl, once wrote, "If you will it, it is no dream." Praying for peace with kavannah is willing it with all your heart. When your prayer helps to make you a peace-loving person, then it truly brings a little more peace into the world.

PRAYERS FOR PEACE
If we truly pray for peace, we will it with all our hearts. If we will it, we find ways to work for it—big ways and small.

6

How God answers

There are two partners in prayer, man and God. We've spoken now about how prayer works on us. It is time to see how God "answers" our prayers.

That is not easy. Talking about God is very difficult and we cannot be certain about what we say. But the Jewish tradition teaches us many things about God that have proved true over thousands of years. And we, too, have a share in this tradition. We have to find our own way to understand God. Jewish prayer and Jewish study aren't just for children. They are for all of us; things we must do throughout our entire life.

Let's begin with a story from the Midrash:

> *When God completed creating the world: the seas and the skies; the sun, moon, and stars; the insects and the birds; the trees, bushes, and flowers; the animals and reptiles, then the angels said to Him, "It is a very lovely world."*

But God replied, "It lacks one thing. It has no voice with which to sing, and so it cannot praise all the beauty."

Then God created man and woman. He gave them souls that they might understand, and voices that they might sing. Now the peoples of the earth can praise the creation of the Lord.

What the rabbis are saying is that God created us in such a way that we would learn to pray to Him. Or to put it another way, God wants us to pray. So all prayers "work," because when we pray we are doing what God wants us to do.

Of course, that brings us to a problem. It sounds funny to say, "God wants . . ." It makes God sound like a person, as if He were some kind of a superman who lives in a place called heaven.

Talking about God

There are many times in our prayerbook when we speak of God in this way. Even the Bible often speaks of God as if He were a man. We talk about our lives being in God's "hand." We call God "King." One prayer begins, "You who hear prayers . . ." Does God have ears?

Many people think that prayer words mean exactly what they say. These people really expect, when they pray, that God will answer them in a beautiful, mellow voice. They think that God can naturally speak English or any other language.

That is surely not what Judaism teaches us. For thousands of years now, our leaders have understood that God is not a man; that He does not have hands, ears, and a mouth the way people do. Just as people and plants are very much alike and yet very different; so God and man are alike and still very different.

Then why did the men of the Bible and the men who wrote our prayerbooks talk of God as if He were a man? Simply because they could think of nothing better in the world to compare God to than to a man. They had to talk about God in some way, and because they also had to talk in the language of human beings, this was the way they chose.

Of course, they talked about God in other ways, too. They called God a "Rock," and it's not hard to imagine why. They were trying to say that God is sure and steady. You can lean and rely upon God. When their enemies threatened them, the men and women of the Bible called God their "Shield."

They also felt that God was close; that He wanted people to do certain things; that He cared what happened to them. Rocks and shields cannot do that. People can. So they used words like "Father" and "King" that helped them to think of God as one who would help them. We will talk about this again, later in the book.

IN TOUCH WITH GOD
Prayer means being in touch with God.
Some prayers bring answers right away.
Other prayers may require us to
wait years for an answer. Meanwhile we can
do our part by staying in touch with God.

But you will have to get used to this way of talking **How** about God if you want to understand the Bible or the **answers** prayerbook. For now, it is important that you see **come** what we mean when we say that God will "answer" prayers. It does not mean that God will open His mouth and say, "Yes" or "No."

Our answers do not come in words. Sometimes they come in a feeling we have when we finish our prayer. And sometimes they come in what happens and how things turn out. Some prayers take a long time to get answered. When we give a name to a new baby, we pray that the baby will grow up to study well, marry well, and act well. We have to wait a long time for an answer to that prayer.

Of course with some prayers, like prayers of thanks or praise or prayers for forgiveness, the answer comes with the prayer itself. We know that God is good. He will accept our thanks and He will be glad to forgive us. The problem with His answers, and most of the questions we have about prayers being answered, has to do with prayers that ask for something.

If you pray for snow to fall in the middle of the month **What kinds** of August when the sun is hot in the sky, would **of answers?** God answer your prayer?

If you are playing baseball and accidentally break a window in your neighbor's house, would God fix the window to answer your prayer?

What kinds of answers can we expect from God?

Prayer not magic

A magician shows his audience one empty hand; he makes a waving motion in the air, speaks a few words, and presto! a little red ball appears between his fingers. It is magic.

Of course, we know that it was just a trick. The magician had practiced it over and over, pulling the little red ball from its hiding place with a thin piece of elastic, until he could do it so fast that only the quickest eye could see the motion. You may have done some magic tricks, too. You know how careful your preparation must be if the trick is to work properly.

But when you were smaller, you might have believed that the red ball really did come right out of the air. You might have believed that the "magic" words made the ball appear. You might even have tried to say the magic words at home to make a red ball appear between your fingers.

Early man often believed that if he said the right words to his god, then his god would be forced to change the world. Some believed that if they knew the right words, God would have to do whatever they told Him to do. Stories like "Aladdin and His Magic Lamp," which speak of genies who are forced to do magic for their owners, are reminders to us today of the way in which more primitive men thought of their gods.

There is a great difference between speaking magic words and saying a prayer. In magic we believe that we can *force* something to happen. In prayer, we know that we are not the boss. In prayer we are trying to "get in touch with" God; not trying to force God to obey us.

As a matter of fact, if God really did obey us, we would not be very happy about it. Imagine what kind of prayers a bully might say, or an army commander who wanted to win a battle, or a man who wanted to hurt another man. We Jews do not believe that God works magic. We believe that God gave us natural laws that do not change, and which even God obeys.

Prayer does not always work in the way we want it to or think that it will. God is concerned with every one of His creatures. In the Psalms it is written:

> You make the grass to grow for the cattle, and the plants for men to cultivate, that he may bring forth food from the earth. How many different things You have created, O Lord. In wisdom have You made them all. They all wait upon You, and You give them their food in due season.

God is concerned about each creature. He listens to the prayers of man, decides with His wisdom whether the prayer is for good or bad, sees whether the prayer will have good or bad results, and then answers the prayer in His own way.

YES OR NO
We Jews believe that God's will is good.
Our prayers say, "May it be Your will."
If the answer is No, we still understand
that God's will for us is good.

How God answers 57

Prayers that will not be answered

The Talmud tells us that God will not answer some kinds of prayer. God will not answer a prayer that is not sincere, a prayer that asks Him to break one of His own laws, a prayer that asks for God to do what we ourselves should be doing, or a prayer that asks God to help us by hurting others.

Let's imagine that in your school there is an essay contest. You want very much to win that contest. If you pray, "Please, God, write a good essay for me," will your prayer be answered? Of course not. But you *could* pray, "Please, God, help me to think of a good idea for my essay, give me inspiration." You do the best you can. You think that you have written a good essay, and so you turn it in. Now would it be good to say a prayer like, "Please, God, don't let that Susy Smarty win this essay contest. She wins all the essay contests. Let me win this time"? Will God answer that prayer?

It is good to ask God for His help whenever we feel that we need it. But when we pray, we should remember how powerful and loving God really is. We should not ask God for petty things like candy bars and chewing gum. We should know how silly it is to pray to God to take the garbage out.

Learning by praying

Yes

Often we learn what kinds of things God will grant us by praying for them. If you have a big test to study for, and instead of studying you watch television and pray to God that He should help you to pass the test, you soon learn that you had better study. God will not do for you what you must do. He is your partner and not your servant.

But sometimes we are not sure if God will help us or not. We are not sure if we are asking for the right thing or if we are asking at the right time, so we say "May it be Your will . . ." or "May our words be acceptable." In a way, we are asking God to show us what He wants by answering these prayers "Yes" or "No."

One of the reasons we have written our prayers down and collected them into a prayerbook is to help us see the kinds of prayers we should pray. In a way the prayerbook shows us the limits of our prayer. Just as the lines or limits on a volleyball field help us to know when a ball has been hit "out," the prayerbook helps us to know what kinds of prayers are right and in order, and what kinds are out of bounds.

Sometimes our prayers are answered, "No." That is truly an answer. God sees much more clearly than man what is good and what is bad. His concern is for the whole universe and He must decide what is good for all of us. And often there are more important things than the ones we want. And sometimes God can see that it is better for us not to get what we want.

More than one answer

Perhaps, using the example of the essay contest, even with all your prayer and hard work someone else wins the contest after all. You might say, "Hah! Now I see that God doesn't answer prayers." Or you might begin writing an essay for the next contest. You might say, "I didn't do well enough. I still have a lot to learn about writing. Help me, God, to be a better writer." If you do the second thing, and go back to work, then maybe your prayer has been answered after all. Would you really want to win something that you did not deserve? Isn't it better when you really do work for it? If you won't stop believing just because the answer is sometimes "No," then prayer will help you to grow and change into a better person.

PRAYING AND WORKING WELL
We do not ask God to set aside His laws,
to give us rewards that we have not earned,
or to favor us at the expense of others.
But we may ask Him to help us do well
in our work and study, to give us strength
and inspiration, to help us understand,
and to go on growing.

The more we pray, the more good reasons we find to pray. We begin to see that there are many things that the world needs and we need that are more important than a new bicycle or a new record. We begin to understand how important everything else in the world is to us and how important and special we are to the world.

We turn to God as a child turns to its father. There are many things we can do without Him, but how much better we do them when we let Him help us! When Jews pray, we see the world in the way that it could be. But to come to that time of peace and of love that we Jews call the End of Days we will have to do our part as God's partners. Prayer and experience teach us what God will do to help, and what we must do for ourselves.

A good reason to pray

the way of Prayer

Lord, God of all the world, Master of the Universe,
Help me so to pray
That by my daily prayers, and by my weekly
    worship,
I may learn my task, the part which I can play
To bring the world a little closer to peace and joy.

Teach me the Jewish tradition
That I may see in the wisdom of the past
A guide to the future.
May I walk the path of Abraham,
    of Isaac and of Jacob, my fathers,
Of Moses and Isaiah, of Akiba and Ben Zakkai,
That I may ever be a blessing
To my father and my mother,
My sisters and my brothers,
To all mankind.

Teach me to make peace, O Eternal Source of Peace.
Amen.

7

Praying together

n the first part of this book we have talked about
vhy it is good for us to pray by ourselves and about
now prayer works. But you must know by now that
he Jewish people has the habit of praying together.
Ne Jews set special times for our services, come
ogether at special places, have special ceremonies
and ways of saying our prayers. We sing and celebrate
ogether.

Now we will see why the Jewish people has come
o believe that it is good to pray together. We will
iee what makes our prayers Jewish. We will talk about
he difference between praying whenever we feel like
t and praying at regular times.

Gathering together to pray is a ceremony that we **We speak**
ews share with many other peoples throughout the **with God**

world. Christians, Muslims, American Indians, even primitive tribes, all have special times set aside when they gather to pray together.

Praying together helps us to remember that we are a part of one people, that we are not alone. Just as it is more fun to play and work beside other people it is more helpful to us when we pray with others. To help us remember that we are not alone, but part of a praying people, Jews have come to speak in prayer of "we" instead of "I."

In the prayer called *Modim*, for example, we say "*We* give thanks unto You, for You are the Lord *our* God and the God of *our* fathers for ever and ever. You are the Rock of *our* lives, *our* saving Shield through every generation." This is only the first line of the Modim and already we have used five words to remind us that we are not alone.

Even when a Jew prays by himself, he is not alone. His prayers remind him of the Jewish people of which he is a part. A Jew praying alone does not change the words of the Shema, when he says: "Hear, O Israel, the Lord is our God, the Lord is One." The Lord is *our* God.

Over and over our prayers remind us that we are a part of the Jewish people, the members of a congregation, using the same words our friends are using. Praying together brings our whole community closer together. It helps us in another way, too.

Being unselfish
When we are alone, we think mostly of ourselves. We say: What do *I* want to do today? What am

doing? Where do *I* want to go? All our feelings are, "*I* want . . ." or "*I* think . . ." or "*I* wish . . ." The same is true of prayer. Leave me alone to pray and I will start talking to God, asking him for what "I" need, or telling Him about what "I" feel.

It is good to do this sometimes, because it helps us to remember that God is our personal helper and partner. But if that is the only kind of praying that we do, then we will soon forget about trying to make our world better. If we always pray by ourselves, then we may soon become selfish and pray only for ourselves.

When we ask for peace, we do not ask just for ourselves. We say:

> *Grant peace, welfare, and blessing, grace and love and mercy, to us; to all Israel, Your people.*

Minyan

Because praying together keeps us from thinking only of ourselves, and because it brings our people closer together as Jews, the rabbis long ago decided to make praying together a regular part of Jewish prayer. They fixed special times, began to set down a special service of prayers, made the synagogue the special place for Jewish prayer and decided that ten Jews should form an official congregation.

We call the ten Jews who form the congregation a *minyan*. The word minyan really means "the count"

or "the numbering," but it is used to mean the ten persons we need for services. Without a minyan, we are not supposed to say the *Borchu*, the Mourner's Kaddish, and certain other prayers. And we do not read the Torah. Of course, if less than ten people are present, they can still pray as individuals. But they are not yet a minyan, and a minyan is entitled to special prayer privileges.

When a minyan is praying, they stand for the whole people of Israel. Of course, the number ten is just a number that we have all agreed upon, but because we agreed upon it so long ago and have been using it for so long, it has become a very strong tradition. In the time of the Talmud in Babylonia, Rabbi Yitzhak must have been thinking of a minyan when he said, "Wherever ten men pray together, God's presence is with them."

In ancient times women were not counted as a part of the ten required for a minyan. Apparently the rabbis were afraid that in their small towns the women would constantly be called away from their homes and children to help make up a minyan. That would cause the whole family to suffer. So the general rule was not to count women as a part of the minyan. Today, some Conservative and all Reform Jews count women as a part of the ten needed to make up a full praying congregation.

Even our prayers seem to gain strength when we are with a group of people. Rabbi Aha, who also lived in the time of the Talmud, explained it this way:

If rich men make a crown for a king, and a poor man comes and gives his share toward the making of it, what does the king say? "Shall I refuse to accept the crown because of this poor man?" The king immediately accepts it and sets it on his head. In the same way, if there are ten good men standing in prayer and a wicked person joins them, what does the Holy One, blessed be He, say? "Shall I refuse to accept their prayer because of this wicked person?" No. All the prayers are accepted.

Old friends

We all know how hard it is to make new friends. When our families move from place to place or when our friends' families move away and we are parted, we become very sad. We will miss our old friends; they have been good to be with.

Prayers can be like old friends, too. Most of our prayers are the same words and sentences that our fathers and grandfathers said. The Shema was spoken by the Jews in the desert when Moses was still leading the people of Israel.

If we stopped using the prayer, *En Kelohenu*, for example, we would probably feel as if we had lost an old friend. When we say

אֵין כֵּאלֹהֵינוּ

There is none like our God.

we are not only saying the words, or singing a melody, but also remembering the many wonderful times when those words have been sung before. In this way, every prayer connects us to the whole history of our people.

The language of faith

Not only do the words of the prayers connect us to the Jewish people, but the language of our prayers does too. Although we can pray to God in any language, and we do, we still use Hebrew in our prayer services. Hebrew is the language of all Israel. Even though Jews are spread all over the world, we can go to any Jewish prayer service anywhere and hear most of the prayers being recited in Hebrew. Using Hebrew helps to remind us that we are one people, all praying for the same things.

Of course, it is important that we understand what we are praying. Without understanding a prayer, we cannot pray it with all our hearts, we cannot pray it with kavannah. So we print our prayerbooks with translations of the Hebrew into our everyday language. Because the words can mean so many different things, there are many different translations of our prayerbooks. And, in addition to translating, we study Hebrew, too, so that we can better understand our daily prayers.

As we study Hebrew, we come to see that we have something in common with Jews all around the world. Hebrew is the language of our people, the language of our Torah, the language of our prayerbook. You could say that Hebrew is a glue that helps us to cling to our Jewishness.

The Mishnah teaches us that the Shema and the Amidah, which are the most important parts of our prayer service, "may be recited in any language." Some parts of our prayer service are not in Hebrew at all, but in Aramaic, a language that is very much like Hebrew. Aramaic was spoken by the Jews of

A PEOPLE OF PRAYER

We Jews are a people of prayer.
The "we" of our prayers links us to our
own Jewish community—and to the great
community of Jewish people praying
in synagogues all over the world.

baruch atah adonai....

Palestine and Babylonia at the time of the Talmud. The Kaddish is one of these Aramaic prayers. And another is the *Kol Nidre* prayer, which we recite on the eve of Yom Kippur.

Jews may pray in any language, but Hebrew will always remain the most beloved language of our faith.

THE HOLY TONGUE
Hebrew is the holy language
of the Jewish people.
It binds all Jews together.
But some of our prayers are in Aramaic.
And Jews may pray in any language.

Of course, you could ask the question, Why should **Using other**
we use other people's prayers? Isn't it better for us **people's**
to make up our own prayers? Wouldn't we have more **words**
kavannah if we used our own words of prayer?

To answer those questions, we have to go back
almost to the beginning. What is our reason for praying? We want to realize that our world is special and
holy. We want to thank God for the gifts that He
has given us, and for His laws that make our lives
better. We want to share with other people the tasks
that need to be done in order to make our world
a place of peace, justice, love, and mercy.

Together as Jews we pray to remind ourselves of
the convenant or contract that we made with God.
We promised to be God's partner in building a good
world.

Saying the prayers together reminds us that we
are not alone. Together, we become less selfish; we
think more of others than ourselves. We remind ourselves that we do not have to bring peace into the
world by ourselves, that many other people, too, are
sharing in that work.

But what about kavannah? Can we really say someone else's words and fill them with kavannah?

In one religion today, that of the Friends, or
Quakers, a prayer service is made up of just the words
that the people wish to speak. Here's how it works:
The Quakers call their service a Prayer Meeting. They
set aside a certain amount of time each week when
they all come together in their meeting house. Silently
they sit waiting. If one of the members feels that
he has something that he wishes to say to God or

to the congregation, then he rises and speaks his prayer. Perhaps his prayer will move someone else to pray. Perhaps not. If no one has anything to say, then everyone sits in silence. After a while, people begin to leave, and the service is over. The greatness of the Quaker prayer service is that everything is based on kavannah. If you don't feel it, you don't do anything. But it has some problems from the Jewish point of view.

Perhaps during the Quaker prayer service someone will rise and address a beautiful prayer to God. His words will be just the words that you would like to say. He will say the things that you feel deep inside of you. At the end, you would say, "Amen," and quietly you might thank him for his prayer, and feel that he was praying for you, too.

But then a sad thing happens. The prayer meeting is over and the words are lost forever. The Quakers will not use the same words again unless someone else happens to say them. And perhaps at the next prayer meeting, if no one says anything that you really think is wonderful, you might wish that you could say those words which you barely remember from before. But they are gone. And soon you forget them altogether.

Then too the people never say anything together. Everyone is always completely on his own. And if you wanted to say something, but did not manage to think of something to say, or did not feel that you had anything important to say, then you would just sit quietly, unable to be a part except to watch and listen.

Now we can see that there are two main reasons that we Jews have for using other people's words as our own prayers. One is to preserve and cherish great prayers as a part of our tradition. And another is to make it possible for us to pray together. Praying together is the first step in the Jewish path toward working together. And working together is the first step toward making our world a better place for all of us.

GREAT PRAYERS OF THE PAST
Praying together reminds us Jews
that we are one people, bound together
to help bring in the world to come.
The great prayers of the past are part
of our tradition. We cherish them.

8

Prayer and poetry

Using poetry in prayer We have seen many ways in which we Jews have learned to make our prayer special. There are still other ways that we have not talked about. One of them is song and the other is the special kind of language we use, poetry.

Even though the prayers in the prayerbook are written out in sentences and paragraphs, so that the prayerbook looks much like any other book, the thoughts are really set down in poetry. And that is true not only for the Hebrew writings, but also for those in English or those translated into English. As a matter of fact, the more like poetry the translation of the Hebrew is, the better it is.

Let's take a prayer that we all know rather well.

First we will write it as it usually appears in a prayer-book:

> And you shall love the Lord your God with all your heart, with all your soul, and with all your might.
>
> And these words which I command you this day shall be upon your heart; and you shall teach them diligently to your children, and you shall talk of them when you sit in your house, and when you walk by the way, and when you lie down, and when you rise up. And you shall bind them as a sign upon your hand, and they shall be like frontlets between your eyes. And you shall write them on the doorposts of your house, and upon your gates.

Now let's write it out as poetry:

> And you shall love
> the Lord your God
> with all your heart,
> with all your soul,
> and with all your might.
>
> And these words, which I command you this day,
> shall be upon your heart;
> and you shall teach them diligently to your children,
> and you shall talk of them
> when you sit in your house,
> and when you walk by the way,
> and when you lie down,
> and when you rise up.
>
> And you shall bind them as a sign upon your hand,
> and they shall be like frontlets between your eyes.
>
> And you shall write them
> on the doorposts of your house,
> and upon your gates.

Now it is easy to see that this prayer is poetry.

In the Hebrew, much of it rhymes. Even in the English translation it has rhythm.

Because most of our prayerbook is written in poetry, we sometimes have to study the prayers before we can understand them. The language of poetry is a little different from the language we use every day. As we are replacing the Torah in the Holy Ark we sing,

It is a tree of life to those who hold it fast, and those who cling to it are made happy. Its ways are ways of pleasantness, and all its paths are peace.

To understand this prayer, we have to know what the words mean when we use them in poetry. For example, we call the Torah a "tree of life." But we know that the Torah is not a tree!

Still, in some ways it is like a tree. Like a tree, its roots going deep, the Torah is planted deep in the heart of the Jewish people. Like a tree, it does not change easily. Like a tree, it makes our world more beautiful. It is living and not dead (remember, it is a "tree of *life*"), which means that it is as important to us today as it was to our forefathers.

When we call the Torah a tree of life, we are using an image, drawing a picture in our minds to help us understand. We talked about such images before, when we spoke of using human terms to describe God. For example, calling God our King.

Poetry is full of images. We talk about "holding fast" to the Torah, but we do not mean grabbing it and hugging it; we mean following its commandments and living by its laws. We say that the Torah has "paths" of peace, but we do not mean that it is like a walk in the country; we mean that if you follow the laws of the Torah, you will walk in peace among your neighbors.

Even the word Torah has become an image in our Jewish prayer-poetry. When we say Torah, we do not always mean the scroll containing the Five Books of Moses, we sometimes mean the whole heritage of the Jewish people, all the words, laws, stories, deeds, and teachings of all the Jews who ever lived and those who are alive now. That is another way in which we think of the word Torah.

That is one of the reasons why we have come to use poetry as our language in prayer: We can say things in poetry that are not everyday facts but that help us to voice our ideas in telling ways.

RHYTHM AND SYMBOL
Many Jewish prayers are written as poetry.
They have rhythm and rhyme in Hebrew.
Even in English they have rhythm.
And we use beautiful figures of speech,
as when we call God our Shield,
or the Torah the Tree of Life.

9

Giving music to our prayers

Another reason for using poetry is that poems are very much like songs. Good poems always seem to sing, as if they had a melody inside of them just waiting to get out. Here is a prayer-poem that already sounds like a song, even before you know a melody for it:

I make pleasant songs, and weave verses,
Because my soul longs for You.
Even as I speak of Your glorious power,
It is Your love my heart desires.
So may all my thoughts be sweet before You,
Because my soul longs for You.

The name of this prayer-poem is *Anim Zemirot,* and it was probably composed as a song.

Of course, music has become an important part of Jewish prayer. We do not have to have it, just as we do not need scenery for a play, but with music our service comes alive. Some melodies have become so precious to us that without them we would feel a great loss. Without the melody for Kol Nidre, for instance, we would lose a very special feeling that we have each year on Erev Yom Kippur, as the cantor asks God to set aside all the promises that we made to Him but could not keep during the past year. The melody helps to make the words special. Nine hundred years ago, the Spanish-Jewish poet, Ibn Ezra, taught that "the words of our prayers are like bodies; the melodies are like souls."

There is a long history to Jewish music. It began when the people of Israel sang a song of victory at the Red Sea:

I will sing to the Lord, for He has won a great victory; horse and rider has He thrown into the sea.

It is continuing today in the modern music of Israel and in the works of great modern Jewish composers.

Song and music played important roles in the days of the Temple. The Levites, helpers of the priests, sang on the steps between the Temple courts; and musical instruments were played inside. The Book of Psalms, which is a collection of prayer-poem-songs written during the time of the Temple, has instructions for which instruments were to be played with certain psalms. Psalm 150 gives us a list of the instruments used:

> Praise Him with the blast of the trumpet,
> Praise Him with the harp and the lyre.
> Praise Him with the drum and the pipe;
> Praise Him with strings and with flute.
> Praise Him with the gong,
> Praise Him with cymbals.
>
> Everything that has breath shall praise the Lord.
> Praise the Lord.

The most famous composer of psalms (the word *psalm* means a prayer-song) was King David. According to the Books of Samuel in the Bible, David first came to the royal court as a musician. He would play the lyre to please King Saul whenever the King suffered from headaches.

David loved music and he loved prayer. Many of the psalms that are in the Book of Psalms were composed by David, and many others were probably written in his honor.

When the Romans destroyed the Second Temple, Jewish services were held in synagogues instead. Now prayers came to replace the animal and harvest sacrifices that were held in the Temple. The people were sad at the destruction of the Temple, and the rabbis decided that we should not use musical instruments at synagogue services on the Shabbat, perhaps because the instruments reminded us too much of the service in the Temple. This rule was especially made about the Sabbath, but in most places it applied to the rest of the week, too. Today, some Conservative Jews and almost all Reform Jews feel that we should use musical instruments on Shabbat because they help us to sing our prayers with kavannah.

MUSIC FOR PRAYERS

Music brings prayers to life. Miriam sang prayers of praise. The Psalms are prayer-poem songs. Musical instruments were used in the Temple. Most Reform and some Conservative congregations use musical instruments today.

Whether or not we use musical instruments, all Jews love to sing their prayers. Our service is filled with songs, and many melodies have been composed for almost every prayer. A good example of this is the prayer *Lechah Dodi*, which we sing to welcome the Sabbath on Friday night. Here is one popular melody:

LE - CHAH DO - DI LIK - RAT KA - LAH, P' NAI SHAB -BAT N' KAB' LAH.

Here is another melody line:

LE - CHAH DO-DI LIK - RAT KA - LAH, P' NAI SHAB - BAT N' KA - B' LAH.

And here is still another:

LECHAH DO-DI LIK-RAT KA - LAH, P' NAI SHAB-BAT N' KAB - LAH. BAT N' KAB' LAH.

The cantor

In the Temple, there had been a class of priests, called *Kohanim,* who conducted the sacrifices and directed whatever prayers were used. But in the synagogues, a custom arose of having one of the congregation lead everyone else in prayer. This man was called the *Sheliah Tsibur*, a "Messenger for the Congregation."

He could be anyone within the congregation, but the Talmud suggests "an elderly man whose youth has been spent decently"; or "one who is modest and agreeable to the people"; or "one who knows how to chant and has a sweet voice."

THE TROP
Here are three words
with the trop shown
in color.

אֵלֶּה תּוֹלְדֹת נֹחַ

In modern times, a part of the job of the Sheliaḥ
Tsibur, the chanting and singing, has become the
job of the *Ḥazan* or cantor. Especially in the last two
hundred years, cantors have devoted themselves to
creating beautiful music for the Jewish prayer service.
Many of these great cantors have left their song-
heritage behind in the form of recorded music.

חַזָּן

We do not know what melodies were used in the
service of the Temple. The systems of writing down
music did not come until much later. But students
of Jewish music believe that the oldest kind of music
we have is the chant by which we read the Torah
and the Haftarah. We call this chant the *trop*. In a
printed Bible, it is shown with small marks that are
added to the Hebrew letters in the same way in which
we add vowels to them. Here is a sample:

Jewish music

אֵלֶּה תּוֹלְדֹת נֹחַ נֹחַ אִישׁ צַדִּיק

These are not notes. They are like little tunes for the
words.

We use one set of tunes for reading the Torah,
and still another for reading the Haftarah portions
that come from the Prophets. We use special chants
for each of the special scrolls read on Holy Days.
And, as if that were not enough, different Jewish
communities worked out different versions of the

chants. The Torah reading sounds different when it is done by a Jew from Iran and when it is done by a Jew from France.

In some congregations, one man does most of the reading from the Torah. He chants the trop as exactly as possible, a job that requires constant study of the Torah. This man is called a *Baal Koray*, a Master of Reading. Like the Ḥazan, his job too came from the original job of the Sheliaḥ Tsibur.

The prayer service has a special chant, too. This chant we call a *Nusaḥ*. There is a Nusaḥ for chanting the daily service, the Shabbat prayer service, a Nusaḥ just for the High Holy Days, and still another for the Festivals. Even the melody for the *Kiddush*, the blessing before wine, changes.

The idea of a Nusaḥ is to create a special mood in which kavannah can come more easily. When we say prayers, we try to say them with meaning; but music helps us to fill our prayers with feeling. We all feel happier with a bright melody to sing, such as the melody of *Sim Shalom* or *Adon Olam*. And we all feel more serious and thoughtful when we hear a melody like the *Kol Nidre*. The melody for the Shema should be majestic and powerful; it should fill us with the majesty and power of our God, the One God. The melody of the *Borchu* should be inviting; it should help us to feel that it is time to pray.

So you see that composing a melody for a prayer is not just a matter of putting together enough notes with enough beats. The melody should fit the prayer, the part of the service in which the prayer comes, and the service as a whole.

When the song fits, then music and words together make the meaning of the prayer clear. Then the music becomes a vital part of the prayer experience. We want to sing that prayer over and over. You might think of the prayer we sing on Erev Shabbat, *Shalom Alechem.* How many times you must have heard that prayer being sung! Now it is like an old friend.

Singing together

Song, like prayer, is best in a group. Music seems to tie people together. Almost everyone enjoys a good song, and almost everyone can sing along. Even in the midst of building a new nation the Israelis have given birth to songs that Jews all around the world have come to love and to sing.

Some Jewish composers have collected folk tunes that the Jews of Europe used to sing, and now that the great Jewish communities of Europe are gone, the songs have been used to write symphonies. In this way, the Yiddish song will never die. One Yiddish song, written in the United States by Sholom Secunda, has become a hit in English. Its name is *Dona Dona.* Because this song deals with the idea of freedom, it is often used as a part of modern religious services.

But the Jews who use music most, and perhaps best, in their prayer-celebrations, are the Ḥasidim. The original Ḥasidim were followers of the Baal Shem Tov, who taught that God could be reached through song and through dance. He and his followers developed a kind of song called a *nigun*. A nigun is a song without words, and the Ḥasidim call the nigun the *highest* kind of song.

כַּוָּנָה

Filling his heart with thoughts of God, the Ḥasid begins to chant his nigun before, during, or after the prayer services; and he tries to forget everything but the melody, and to fill the melody with his deepest prayers.

The most important thing is—kavannah.

Today, Ḥasidic songs have become very popular among Jews. There are even modern composers who try to write songs in the pattern of the Ḥasidic nigun.

There are two other kinds of Jewish singing that we have not yet talked about. One of them is the rich prayer and song heritage of the Oriental Jews. In Israel collectors have recorded these prayer-and-song melodies so that they will not be lost.

Another source of Jewish prayer-song is our own American-Jewish community. Many new prayer-songs have been written recently by young American Jews: Orthodox, Conservative, and Reform. Some of these prayer melodies have been recorded as songs, others have been recorded as part of "rock" services or jazz services or just "modern" prayer services.

Really we are doing just what the author of one of the psalms wished us to do. He said, "Sing to the Lord a new song." Bringing new music to the

words of the prayerbook helps to make the words
live for us.

OLD SONGS AND NEW
Jews have many melodies for prayers
and blessings. The prayer service has a
special chant, a Nusaḥ. Even the Haftarah
is chanted.

10

The berachah

The most common Jewish prayer is the berachah, or blessing. You probably already know many *berachot,* you have said them many times. The prayer over bread is a berachah; the prayer over wine is a berachah; the prayer over the Sabbath and Festival candles is a berachah, too.

Each of these prayers begins with the same six words. Only the end is different for each. The Talmud tells us that the men of the Great Assembly began the use of the berachah. (The Great Assembly was made up of groups of men who met in Jerusalem between 500 and 200 B.C.E. They were the leaders of the Jewish people after Ezra died and a sort of Jewish Congress to pass laws for our people.) They also decided which books should be added to the Torah, as a part of the Bible (for example, Esther

88

and Daniel were added by them). They started the custom of reading the Torah to the people on Mondays, Thursdays, and Saturdays. And they set up the basic rules of a synagogue service. But as the first step in creating the service, and as the first step in helping the Jews to create a special way of praying, the men of the Great Assembly gave us a "formula," the berachah.

A formula is a particular way of doing something. **A formula** The simplest formula is one that tells you all you need to know, such as a recipe for baking a cake. It not only tells you what to do to make a cake, but tells you the proper order for making it. That is important. If your mother lined up all the ingredients for a cake in front of you, you still might not be able to bake a cake. And if you confuse the order in cooking, things can turn out pretty badly. That is where the recipe is important.

Of course, after you have baked a lot of cakes, you discover that they can be pretty much the same. They take flour, eggs, sugar. But you can change the flavoring or the icing. It may still look like a yellow cake, but it may taste like an orange cake, or a pineapple cake. It may have white icing that tastes like vanilla or brown icing that tastes like chocolate.

Formulas are good because they tell us what to do and in what order to do it. But sometimes we need to change a formula to make exactly what we want.

The men of the Great Assembly saw that our prayer needs change, too. They made the berachah an "open formula." The first six words are fixed and regular. They have certain ideas and they go in a certain order, but what follows is open. You fill it in depending on what you are thanking God for at that moment.

First, we'll talk about the regular six words of the berachah, and then we will talk about the words that Jews have added to them in the past.

Here is the basic berachah formula, without translation because we want to talk about each word:

בָּרוּךְ אַתָּה יְיָ. אֱלֹהֵינוּ מֶלֶךְ הָעוֹלָם

Baruch Atah Adonai Elohenu Melech ha-Olam . . .

Six words The word *Baruch* is one of the best known words in the Hebrew language. Believe it or not, we cannot agree on a translation for this word. One translation is "Blessed," and another is "Praised." The word Baruch may come from the Hebrew word that means "knee." Then it would remind us that when we say a berachah we are, in a way, bending our knees to God.

Of course, when we think of bowing or bending our knees, we think of a king. This is the way in which people show a king that they give him their loyalty and their service. And that is what we do when we say a berachah to God. The word Baruch helps us to remember that we are God's servants.

The word *Atah,* which means "You," is even more important. This word tells us a great deal about how we Jews think of our God. We speak to God as if He were a person. We call him "You." We can think of God as our Partner and Friend. No matter how busy our Friend may be, He will still have time to listen to us. We can talk directly to God in this way, too. To show this, we use the word Atah.

Let's talk about the next two words together. They are an interesting combination—*Adonai Elohenu.* The second word, *Elohenu,* is easy to translate. It means "Our God." It is a general word for God. In English we start the word with a capital "G" when we are speaking of the real God, and with a small "g" when we are speaking of idols. The Bible has the same kind of trick. Whenever this word is used about the real God, it is usually as a plural, *Elohim.*

But here and often, it says "our God." Of course, He doesn't just belong to us. Other people believe in our God, too. But our forefathers were the first to know clearly that He was the One God of all the world. They passed that belief on to their children and made it the basic faith of the Jewish people. So we feel especially close to Him after all these years and we call Him "our God."

A FORMULA FOR BLESSING
The berachah is a formula.
It always begins the same way.
We address God as "You" (Atah)
but we do not forget
that He is King
of the universe (Melech ha-Olam).

God has a name, says the Bible. This time it is not a word that can be used for anything else. It is His very own name. But it would not be good for us to call God by His name constantly, for that would seem too familiar, almost insulting. So we Jews have an old rule. Whenever we see the four letters that make up God's own name יְהֹוָה or the two letters that stand for them יְיָ –we pronounce instead, אֲדֹנָי "Lord," as a servant would say to his master. This reminds us that God is our master; it is respectful. So *Adonai* means "Lord."

A Midrash tells us that the reason Adonai always comes before Elohenu is because Adonai stands for God's mercy, while Elohenu stands for God's justice. We like to think of our God as a God of mercy, first.

The Midrash goes on to tell the story of a king who had a new drinking glass. Two drinks were brought to the king. One was a wine so hot that the king was afraid that if he poured it into his new glass, the glass would shatter from the sudden heat.

But the other wine was ice cold; and the king knew that cold, too, could crack a glass. So the king poured both drinks at once into his new glass and the glass was saved.

Mercy, the Midrash tells us, is like the hot drink and justice like the cold one. When the Lord God wished to create the world, the Midrash says, He considered first what He should do. If God made it only of justice then people would always be sinning by mistake . . . But if He filled it with mercy alone, people would never stop sinning because they would know that God would forgive them no matter what they did. So God wisely chose to use an equal measure of both—mercy and justice—and thus the world survived.

The last two words of the formula are *Melech ha-Olam*, "King of the universe . . ." A moment before we spoke directly to God as Atah. Now we remind ourselves that we are not standing beside a chum. The Lord, our God, is the one and only God of all creation. He fixed its patterns and its rules, from the tiniest atoms to the greatest stars whirling in the galaxies. His power runs it all, and He is greater than any part of His creation. We are not just saying thanks to the sun or the moon or the wind, but to the Lord, God of all.

How can we translate the six words all together to make sense now? There are many ways. One is "Blessed art thou, O Lord our God, King of the universe . . ." Another is "We praise You, O Lord our God, King of the universe . . ." And still another is "Praise be to You, O Lord our God, King of the universe . . ."

BLENDING MERCY WITH JUSTICE
Adonai stands for God's mercy.
Elohenu stands for His justice.
We use these words together.
In Jewish law and teaching
justice is blended with mercy,
like cold wine with hot.

No matter how we translate it, we can see now how it works. In these first few words, we have come to understand that we are servants and partners of God, that God is both our King and our friend. We say the berachah to remind us that we cannot do anything alone, that we depend on God's help; and to thank God for the help which He gives us.

Berachot The berachot were designed to help us see that everything in the world is special and sacred to us. Let's see how Jews have used the berachah formula through the ages.

One thing that we all do is to get up every morning. Here are some berachot that the rabbis said we should say every morning. (These prayers are supposed to be said at home, but now they are also a part of the traditional synagogue service.)

Blessed are You, O Lord our God, King of the universe,
who did not make me a slave.

One of the first ways in which God helped you was in choosing the time and place you were born. If you had been born in almost any other century or even in other places today, you might very well have been a slave. Instead, you are a free person, free to make choices about what you want to do with your life. Saying this blessing every morning should make you feel good as it reminds you of how lucky you are.

We are lucky in other ways, too. Not only were we born into freedom, but we were given bodies which support our life. The rabbis knew long ago how wonderful the human body really is. Here is the berachah they wrote to thank God for our bodies:

> We praise You, O Lord our God, King of the universe, who have formed man in wisdom, and created in him many tubes and openings. It is well known before You, that if only one of these be opened, or only one of these be closed, it would be impossible to exist and stand before You. Blessed are You, O Lord, who are the wondrous healer of all flesh.

Since God created the laws of nature, the rabbis ended this prayer with thanks to God for providing ways for our flesh to mend itself. Did you ever stop to think that one of the most wonderful things about you is the almost magical way that the body cleans itself, cuts heal themselves, broken bones mend, and bruises go away?

We can see from this blessing that a Jew should try to stay healthy so that he can "stand" before God. That is, if we do not try to stay healthy and strong, we do not serve God or our community very well.

VARYING THE FORMULA

We may vary the berachah formula to fit the occasion. We may bless or praise God that we have been born free, not slaves, that our bodies are wonderfully made, that we recover from sickness, that broken bones mend—and a cast may, at last, be laid aside.

11

A formula for mitzvot

Whenever we are about to perform a *mitzvah*, one of the commandments that we were given in the Torah, we say a longer form of the berachah formula to remind us that we are serving God. The words we add are these:

אֲשֶׁר קִדְּשָׁנוּ בְּמִצְוֹתָיו. וְצִוָּנוּ

. . . Asher kidshanu b'mitzvotav v'tzivanu . . .

Now the berachah says "We praise You, O Lord our God, King of the universe, who have made us holy by Your commandments and commanded us to. . ."

Of course, we all recognize this longer berachah formula from the blessing over the Sabbath or Ḥanukkah candles. Another example of this special formula is the berachah we say when we are placing a *mezuzah* on our doorpost for the first time.

The commandment to place a mezuzah is in the first paragraph after the Shema, where we are commanded to "write [the commandments] on the doorposts of your house and upon your gates." To keep this mitzvah, we have invented a small container called a mezuzah, in which we place a little piece of parchment. On the parchment is written the Shema prayer and two paragraphs from the Bible that tell of our love for God and for His commandments. When we put up a mezuzah for the first time, we say:

> We praise You, O Lord our God, King of the universe, who have made us holy by Your commandments and commanded us to affix the Mezuzah.

Most of the mitzvot have been given to us to make our lives richer, and to help guide us on our path to peace and brotherhood. You might ask how the mezuzah can help us. To understand, we have to know how the mezuzah can be used once it is in place on the doorpost of our house.

As we go into the house with a mezuzah on the door, we reach up and touch the mezuzah with our fingertips. It reminds us that we should behave as Jews in the house which we are entering. And as

THE LONGER BERACHAH
We use a longer berachah formula
before performing any mitzvah.
We remind ourselves in this way that the
goodness of the mitzvah comes from God,
who commanded us to perform it.

we leave the house, we touch the mezuzah again, this time to remind us that we should behave as Jews everywhere in God's world.

Saying berachot together

So far, we have been talking about what happens when you say a berachah. But there is more to the Jewish formula! If you are listening as someone else says a berachah, there are two things for you to do.

When the person praying comes to God's name, Adonai, we are expected to say בָּרוּךְ הוּא וּבָרוּךְ שְׁמוֹ: "Praised be He, and praised be His name." In this way we show that we have heard the Lord's name, and we cannot let that pass without adding our own word of thanks and praise.

And when the berachah is complete, we are expected to say אָמֵן *Amen*. Exactly what this word means is hard to say. Usually we use it to mean "Hold fast," or "Believe." Somehow it came to be used as a word which helps us to join in someone else's berachah. We do not know where the word came from, but the first time it appears is in the book of Numbers and in Deuteronomy it is already a response to a prayer.

Many people have tried to explain where the word Amen came from. One nice interpretation is that Amen is really an abbreviation made up of the first three letters of the Hebrew sentence אֵל מֶלֶךְ נֶאֱמָן:

AGREEING
When someone else says a berachah, we join in.
When he says "Adonai," we say "Praised be He, and praised be His name." And at the end we say, "Amen"—"So be it."
We remind ourselves through the berachot of God's part in the world—and of our role in helping make this a more friendly world.

Amen

that means "God is a faithful King." But wherever the word Amen came from, today we use it to mean "So be it!" or "I believe that, too!" and to show that we agree with the person who is saying the berachah.

When we pray, we try to make our world seem a little more special. We try to remember that we are partners with God and that we must do our share in making the world a better place. The berachot help us in this.

Knowing how good it makes a person feel when his world is a special place, the rabbis told us that we should try to find reasons to say a hundred berachot each day! What they meant was that we should keep our lives as holy and sacred as we could. In the Bible, the same idea is said in another way, "You shall be holy, for I the Lord your God am holy."

Because we are supposed to say the berachot all day long, whenever and wherever we can, the berachot help to remind us all day of God's place in the world. And they help us to remember that every moment is special and sacred.

The berachot tie us to our people, too. Even when we are not saying a berachah, when someone else does, we pause and join in. In a way, the berachot remind us of our people and how our people serve the Lord and one another.

And, because they are short formulas, they do not make any great demands on us. The berachot are an easy way we have of reminding ourselves that our real task is to make our world into a world of peace in every way we can.

12

Other ways of prayer

Jews have been composing prayers for as long as the Jewish people has existed, and not all of these prayers fit into the berachah formula. Not all of these prayers are found in our prayerbook, either. If they were, our prayerbook would be many volumes and look like an encyclopedia.

Now let us look at some prayers that do not fit into the berachah formula and some that are very much like berachot. They come from many different places and times; and they speak of many different ideas.

Praying aloud You might try reading some of these prayers aloud. When you read something out loud you bring more to it: you use your eyes, your ears, your lips, and your mind. In other words, you usually have a better chance of reaching kavannah when you bring yourself to actually say something aloud.

SEEING AND ENJOYING

Blessed be He who did not let His world lack anything, but created for it beautiful creatures and goodly trees, that men might see them and enjoy them.

Have you seen a giant redwood or a shining golden lion? Or a butterfly? Or a sapling rising from the earth? Without these our world would not be the wondrous place we know. Even in the barren desert, creatures and plants learn to live and flourish. They remind us of the mystery of life. And most wondrous of all, when God creates, each creation is unique, no two are alike.

The Midrash reminds us that when we make coins, we make them from a mold. Every coin is like the one made before it, and just like the one made afterward. In a way, God makes man from a mold, too. We say that God makes man in His own image. But each man is altogether different from every other.

This prayer, which is supposed to be said when we see something beautiful, reminds us of the miracle of creation. The beauty around us is not just there. It is God's special gift. We should stop a moment to thank God for it.

Love for God

IF YOU HAD CATTLE

Master of the universe!
People pay me to watch their cows.
You know that if You had cows
and gave them to me to watch over them,
from You I would take no pay,
because I love You.

"If You Had Cattle" is the prayer of a simple man. Still, it is a beautiful prayer because it says so much with so few words. What feeling do you discover when you read this prayer? Can you feel the love that the simple man has for God?

The rabbis have said that there is a time for long prayers and a time for short prayers. Do you think that making this prayer longer would make it better?

Prayer-games   The next prayer is a kind of prayer-game.

YOU AND I

O God, my God,
You are the Master and I am the servant.
 Who cares for the servant, except the Master?
You are God and I am man.
 Who cares for man, except God?
You are the Living and I am the dying.
 Who cares for the dying, except the Living?
You are the Potter, and I am the clay.
 Who cares for the clay, except the Potter?
You are the Shepherd and I am the sheep.
 Who cares for the sheep, except the Shepherd?
You are the Listener and I am the talker.
 Who cares for the talker, except the Listener?
You are the Beginning and I am the end.
 Who cares for the end, except the Beginning?

MANY KINDS OF PRAYERS
Some prayers are very old. Others have been given new forms. Some are prayer-games, like acrostics.

Can you add some of your own ideas to this prayer? Could you write a prayer-game of your own?

People have often tried to write prayer-games. Some of these games used patterns like having the first letter of each line begin with a different letter of the Hebrew *alef-bet*. That is called an acrostic. Acrostic prayer-games go back to the time of the Bible.

The most famous acrostic in the prayerbook is the *Ashre* (the name comes from the first word and means, "Happy"), which is Psalm 145 plus two lines from other psalms. Each line of this poem is a prayer in itself. Some lines are praises to God, but others are reminders to man. Here are a few of its lines in English:

> *The Lord upholds all who fall . . . The Lord is near to all who call to Him in truth . . . . The eyes of all look hopefully to You, O Lord . . . . You open Your hand and satisfy every living thing . . .*

Here are four lines of the Ashre in Hebrew, showing the beginning of the Hebrew alef-bet.

אָ רוֹמִמְךָ אֱלוֹהַי הַמֶּלֶךְ   וַאֲבָרְכָה שִׁמְךָ לְעוֹלָם וָעֶד:
בְּ כָל־יוֹם אֲבָרְכֶךָ   וַאֲהַלְלָה שִׁמְךָ לְעוֹלָם וָעֶד:
גָּ דוֹל יְיָ וּמְהֻלָּל מְאֹד   וְלִגְדֻלָּתוֹ אֵין חֵקֶר:
דּ וֹר לְדוֹר יְשַׁבַּח מַעֲשֶׂיךָ   וּגְבוּרֹתֶיךָ יַגִּידוּ:

Sometimes an acrostic was "signed" by the man
who wrote it. Instead of using the letters of the alef-
bet to begin each new line, he used the letters of
his own name. Could you write a prayer that way?

Prayers in Aramaic   Not all prayers were originally written in Hebrew.
One of the most beautiful prayers of Judaism, the
Kaddish, was written in Aramaic, the language spoken
by the common people of Israel at the time this prayer
was composed. In the beginning, this prayer was
used as a way to praise God. Later, even though
it does not mention death, the Kaddish came to be
recited by mourners during the year following the
death of a relative, and each year on the anniversary
of that death.

In some congregations, particularly among Reform
Jews, the whole congregation says the Mourner's
Kaddish together. Here is the Mourner's Kaddish in
Aramaic, with its translation:

יִתְגַּדַּל וְיִתְקַדַּשׁ שְׁמֵהּ רַבָּא. בְּעָלְמָא דִּי־בְרָא כִרְעוּתֵהּ.
וְיַמְלִיךְ מַלְכוּתֵהּ. בְּחַיֵּיכוֹן וּבְיוֹמֵיכוֹן. וּבְחַיֵּי דְכָל־בֵּית
יִשְׂרָאֵל. בַּעֲגָלָא וּבִזְמַן קָרִיב. וְאִמְרוּ אָמֵן:

Raise high and glorify the name of God
throughout the world He created by His will.
May He build His kingdom in your life,
During your days
And during the life of all the House of Israel,
Soon, and in a time close at hand.
So let us say, Amen.

יְהֵא שְׁמֵהּ רַבָּא מְבָרַךְ. לְעָלַם וּלְעָלְמֵי עָלְמַיָּא:
יִתְבָּרַךְ. וְיִשְׁתַּבַּח. וְיִתְפָּאַר. וְיִתְרוֹמַם. וְיִתְנַשֵּׂא. וְיִתְהַדָּר.
וְיִתְעַלֶּה. וְיִתְהַלָּל. שְׁמֵהּ דְּקֻדְשָׁא
בְּרִיךְ הוּא.
לְעֵלָּא מִן־כָּל־בִּרְכָתָא. וְשִׁירָתָא. תֻּשְׁבְּחָתָא. וְנֶחֱמָתָא.
דַּאֲמִירָן בְּעָלְמָא. וְאִמְרוּ אָמֵן:

Let the name of the Holy One,
Blessed be He,
Be praised and glorified,
Be exalted, raised up, and honored,
Be magnified and spread;

Though we know
He is above all praises,
And above all songs of praise,
And above all blessings,
And all kind words spoken in our world.
Even so, we say, Amen.

יְהֵא שְׁלָמָא רַבָּא מִן־שְׁמַיָּא. וְחַיִּים. עָלֵינוּ וְעַל־כָּל־
יִשְׂרָאֵל. וְאִמְרוּ אָמֵן:

Let peace pour from the heavens,
With life for us and for all Israel.
Let us say, Amen.

עוֹשֶׂה שָׁלוֹם בִּמְרוֹמָיו. הוּא יַעֲשֶׂה שָׁלוֹם. עָלֵינוּ וְעַל־
כָּל־יִשְׂרָאֵל. וְאִמְרוּ אָמֵן:

Creator of peace in His high places,
May He create peace for us
And for all Israel.
For this, we say, Amen.

Many people believe that the Kaddish is a very comforting prayer: that it helps to make us feel better in times of sorrow. From what you read, can you tell why?

THE KADDISH
The Kaddish was written in Aramaic. It is
said by mourners, but does not mention death.
It glorifies God, and looks forward
to the time of God's kingdom.

Sometimes we write a new prayer using an old one **New prayers** as a model. There are many reasons for changing **from old** a prayer. Sometimes the way we think changes. Sometimes the words grow old and lose their meaning and we forget what the prayer is really about. Sometimes a prayer is changed so that we can understand it in a new way.

Usually prayers get changed when a new prayerbook is printed, or a new translation of the old prayerbook is made. *The Union Prayerbook* gives us a good example of how a prayer can be changed and become more beautiful in its new form. First, here is the old prayer from a traditional prayerbook:

> *Grant peace, welfare, blessing, grace, lovingkindness and mercy unto us and unto all Israel, Thy people. Bless us, O our Father, even all of us together, with the light of Thy countenance; for by the light of Thy countenance Thou hast given us, O Lord our God, the Torah of life, lovingkindness and righteousness, blessing, mercy, life and peace; and may it be good in Thy sight to bless the people Israel at all times and in every hour with Thy peace.*

Now here is the new prayer that was made from the traditional one:

> *Grant us peace, Thy most precious gift, O Thou eternal source of peace, and enable Israel to be its messenger unto the peoples of the earth. Bless our country that it may ever be a stronghold of peace, and its advocate in the council of nations. May contentment reign within its borders, health and happiness within its homes. Strengthen the bonds of friendship and fellowship among the inhabitants of all lands. Plant virtue in every soul, and may the love of Thy name hallow every home and every heart. Praised be Thou, O Lord, Giver of peace.*

This new prayer was written in English. Really, prayers can be written in any language.

Of course, changing the prayers in the prayerbook is not a new thing. At all times and in all places, Jews have changed the prayerbook to make it more meaningful to them. We Jews have ever been a praying people. That is one reason why there are so many different kinds of Jewish prayer.

Now, let's end this chapter with a beginning for you. Why not make your day start in a special, Jewish way? This is a prayer which Jews have been saying first thing in the morning for centuries. It is called the *Modeh Ani,* "I give thanks."

מוֹדֶה אֲנִי לְפָנֶיךָ. מֶלֶךְ חַי וְקַיָּם.
שֶׁהֶחֱזַרְתָּ בִּי אֶת־נִשְׁמָתִי בְּחֶמְלָה. רַבָּה אֱמוּנָתֶךָ:

I give thanks to You, O living and eternal King, who have restored my soul to me in mercy: great is Your faithfulness.

13

A place of prayer

To teach us how important the synagogue was, our sages, the men who wrote the Talmud, once told us this legend. If a man usually comes to the synagogue, and one day he fails to appear for some reason, then God himself asks, "Where is my faithful one?"

Why should the synagogue be so important to God? Can't we pray anywhere? Isn't our prayer just as worthwhile if we say it in a field or if we whisper it on a crowded bus?

The answer is yes. It is just as worthwhile a prayer. But setting aside a regular place of prayer helps us to remember to pray regularly. And our synagogue is more than just a place of prayer. In a way, we fill our synagogues with our greatest hopes and dreams, with our prayers and our studies, with our past, our present, and our future.

The synagogue Synagogues were not always buildings with a sanctuary and a religion school wing. Sometimes Jews met in someone's house to pray or even in a store. Sometimes they met in caves or basements, and sometimes in an open field. Jews can pray anywhere that is clean, and anytime that they have a minyan.

Of course, the larger our community grows, the more difficult it is to find a place for us to meet together. So Jews have found it best to build a special place and we call it a synagogue. The word *synagogue* is Greek, and it is a name used for 2,000 years, ever since Jews lived in Greek-speaking countries. It means "a place to come together." In Hebrew, we call the synagogue by three names.

The first name is *Bet ha-Knesset*, which means a place where people gather together, a meeting place. When we have a meeting of the youth group, or of the Sisterhood or Brotherhood of the congregation, or when the synagogue holds an art show, or shows a film, or has a guest speaker, we are using it as a Jewish House of Meeting, a Bet ha-Knesset.

But it is more than that, too. In Yiddish, the name for a synagogue is *shul*, "school." In Hebrew we show the same idea when we call our synagogue a *Bet ha-Midrash*, a "House of Study." When you come to religion school at your synagogue, you are turning it into a Bet ha-Midrash. Most synagogues have adult classes, too, where your parents may come to study.

We also call our synagogue a House of Prayer, or *Bet ha-Tefillah*. The Talmud tells us that "Inside the synagogue, a man's prayer is heard. . . ." And much of the time we spend together in the synagogue is spent in prayer.

We get a special kind of feeling when we enter the synagogue. It is a building which really belongs to us all. We think of it as a House of God, and as we use it properly that is just what it becomes. It is a place which we have filled with our study, our thought, our feelings, our prayers, and our actions. In a way, the synagogue is a part of us, the way a good friend is a part of us.

The synagogue is a special place, one set aside for us to meet our people and our God. Since it means so much to us, we try to make it remind us of our traditions, and of the Jewish task of working for peace.

Inside the synagogue

We have always tried to make our synagogues beautiful, too. When a place is beautiful, it is easier to have kavannah in it. Places that are dark or dirty bother us. They make it more difficult to turn to God—though sometimes those are just the places where we need to feel God's presence most. When we are building a synagogue today, we spend much time thinking about how it should look. We want each piece of the decorations to remind us of our people or of God. We want our Holy Ark, the place where we store the Torah scrolls, to be beautiful inside and out. We want our classrooms to be cheerful, so that we can better study with kavannah. We try to make our synagogue a place that will help us, a place where our thoughts will be free.

OUR SYNAGOGUE

We call our synagogue by many names: meeting place, school, House of Study, House of Prayer. We try to make it a beautiful place.

Symbols in our synagogues

We also try to fill our synagogues with things that are special for us. We call these things *symbols*. A symbol is a thing that reminds us of something else —of something greater than itself. For example, a ribbon may remind you that you won first place in a relay race. Or a patch may remind you that you have earned a special rank in the scouts. The Jewish people has many symbols, too, to remind us Jews of our heritage.

You could probably name most of the symbols of the sanctuary, because you see them all the time. They are there to help us remember how and why we have come to this synagogue.

Our synagogues are symbols, too. They are built in a way to remind us of the ancient Temple in Jerusalem. The traditional rule is to build them so that when we pray, the congregation is facing in the direction of Jerusalem. But some of our symbols are even older than the time of the First Temple. Some of them go back to the time when the Children of Israel were wanderers in the desert.

You remember the Torah story. The laws that God gave Moses on Mount Sinai were written on two stone tablets, in Hebrew the *Luḥot ha-Berit*, the Tablets of the Covenant. Most synagogues have the symbol of the two tablets somewhere near the ark. Sometimes they are plain, but more often they will have the Ten Commandments or the first word of each commandment on them. Seeing this symbol reminds us of the kind of life Jews should lead.

When Moses gave the *Luḥot ha-Berit* to the people, they needed a place to keep the tablets. So they designed an ark to carry with them through the desert. The ark was like a small chest with long wooden poles extending out at the front and at the back so that it could be carried. Even in the earliest synagogues that our archaeologists have found, the *Aron Kodesh*, the Holy Ark, is at the front of the sanctuary where it can easily be seen. Here we keep our Torah scrolls and any other scrolls, like the book of Esther, which we read on special occasions.

When we pray, we face toward the Aron Kodesh. When it is open, we stand to show our respect for the scrolls of the Torah. We are not worshiping the scrolls. They are only books and we Jews do not worship them. But they are holy books, the holiest we know. They teach us about God and our duties to Him. So whenever we are in the synagogue, we are reminded that the holiest thing is to do what God asks us to.

Moses wanted another special symbol for the place where the people prayed, too. So he commanded

מְנוֹרָה

Bezalel, a great artist, to make a seven-branched oil lamp. We call it the *Menorah*. Today, we try to display some sort of menorah in our synagogues to remind us of how long our people has been faithful to God. And today, too, the menorah has a new meaning, for it is also the symbol of the new Jewish State of Israel.

(The Hebrew word *menorah* means "lamp." It can be used for a lamp with any number of oil bowls. So we use the same word for the seven-branched oil lamp of Bezalel and also for the eight-branched candlestick of Hanukkah. Israelis, to make things clearer, have invented a special word for the Hanukkah menorah, they call it a *Hanukkiah*.)

The seven branches of the menorah remind us of the seven days of the creation story; and the middle branch reminds us of the Sabbath. In the ancient Temple, the center branch was always kept lit. Today, we have the symbol of the *Ner Tamid*, an "Eternal Light." It hangs over the Aron Kodesh and is such a lovely symbol that artists have made many different designs for it. And people have found many different meanings in the Ner Tamid, too. Some have said that it reminds us of the Sabbath, which is Israel's constant light. Others say that it reminds us of God's constant watchfulness over the people of Israel.

In the Temple, there was an altar for making animal sacrifices and grain sacrifices. Today in the synagogue there are no sacrifices, but we do build a *Bimah* in the sanctuary. Traditionally, the Bimah was in the center of the sanctuary and the people sat all around it. Sephardic synagogues are still built

בִּימָה

this way today. One of the nice things about having it this way was the parade that took place whenever the Torah was taken from the Aron Kodesh to be read. Today most synagogues place the Bimah up front with the Aron Kodesh.

Symbols in the Aron Kodesh

Just as we decorate our synagogue to remind us of the beauty of God's world and of our heritage, we decorate our Torah scrolls to remind us of the beauty of God's laws. The *Sefer Torah*, "Torah Scroll," is the holiest thing that we Jews have. We honor it in many ways. We place a cloth mantle over it to keep it from dust and dirt. The cloth is generally a rich one like velour plush or satin, and it is often decorated with figures or sayings. Some say the mantle reminds us of the robe that the high priest wore in the Temple.

The scroll itself has wooden poles at each end. We call each *Etz Hayyim*, "Tree of Life." That probably comes from the prayer that says that our Torah is a "tree of life to those who hold on to it." It is nice to think of a book giving life to us.

Our rabbis taught us that in Judaism there are three great honors or "crowns"—the crown of being a priest, the crown of being a king, and the crown of being a student of Torah. And of the three crowns, they said, the crown of Torah is the greatest. Jews sometimes decorate the Torah by placing a *Keter*, a crown, on top of the wooden poles of the Sefer Torah.

Since that is very expensive, we are more likely to decorate each pole with a silver ornament which

רִמּוֹן

יָד

חֹשֶׁן

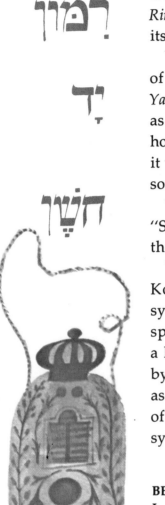

we call a "pomegranate" using the Hebrew word *Rimmon*. This ornament probably got its name from its shape. The Rimmon, too, has crowns on its top.

We also add two other symbols to the dressing of the Torah scroll. One is a pointer that we call a *Yad*, a "Hand." We use it to follow along in the text as we are reading from the Torah. The scroll is too holy for us to go running our fingers over it. Besides it would not be long before we smeared the ink and soiled the parchment.

The other symbol is a *Hoshen*, a "Breastplate" or "Shield." It reminds us of the breastplate worn by the high priest during services in the Temple.

With all of these symbols, the symbols in the Aron Kodesh and the symbols all around us in the synagogue, we remind ourselves that this is a very special place. We have set aside our sanctuary to be a house of Israel, a place where we are surrounded by our people and its symbols. And we have set it aside, too, as a House of God, where we are reminded of God's laws and of His love. In this way all the symbols help us to concentrate our attention and our

BEAUTIFUL SYMBOLS
In honoring the Torah scrolls
we honor God. We follow the text
with a Yad, or Hand.
To show our great reverence,
a crown is placed on top
of the poles of the Torah scrolls.

kavannah on our prayers, for no matter what way we turn in the sanctuary the symbols call to us to remember.

Today some synagogues are called temples. Of course the word Temple (notice the capital "T") really means the Temple in Jerusalem that Solomon built, or the one that replaced it after the First Temple was destroyed. But some Jews want to point out that anywhere Jews are, the spirit of the ancient Temple is with them. And because the synagogue carries on for the Temple, they call it a Temple.

Temple or synagogue?

Other Jews prefer to say synagogue. They believe that "Temple" should be a special name only for the place in Jerusalem spoken of in the Bible. There has been no Temple in Jerusalem for about 2,000 years. But many Jews want to save the word Temple to remember in a special way the place where our forefathers worshiped.

Our synagogues can teach us much about what it means to be Jewish. Whether we come to worship in our own synagogue, or we enter a synagogue in a far-away country, we immediately feel the peacefulness of the sanctuary. We find the symbols that we know and love, symbols that fill us with memories of the history of our people. It seems as if the sanctuary were filled with the most beautiful thoughts of all the people who had prayed in it. And all those beautiful thoughts of peace and love, friendship and kindness, goodness and mercy, gather around us as we pray and remind us of the kind of prayers that we want to say.

PEACE and JUSTICE

O God!
May I ever learn to find my place among the people
Israel.
May my heart be a Jewish heart, my mind a Jewish
mind, my soul a Jewish soul;
May all my actions bring a good name to the word Jew.

May the works of my hand and the ideas I design
Be kind and gentle.
May I find my home in the House of Prayer,
My life in the tasks You have given to Your people,
My words in the words You have spoken and the words
spoken truly in Your name,
My deeds in the mitzvot You have commanded.

May Your law rule over all the earth; and justice and
mercy be Your kingdom everlasting.
May the Messiah come soon and in my day, bringing
peace and hope to all.
And may I take my place beside those who love and
serve You.

Amen

14

Putting it all together

Having all the parts to something is not quite like
having the whole thing put together. Imagine opening a Ḥanukkah present and finding inside a wind-up
key, a few springs and coils of metal, two pieces
of aluminum, some pegs and brads, a few metal posts,
some small rubber wheels, and two axles—but no
diagram, no instructions to tell you how to put it
all together! What a gift!

That is very different from receiving a toy car that
you can simply wind up and off it goes. Of course,
they really are the same: without the parts, we could
not have the car. But the parts must be put together
in just the right way if they are to work.

That is about where we are in our study of prayer.
We know almost all the parts of Jewish prayer; now
we need to put them together so that we can see
how they work.

Perhaps the prayerbook should come with instructions. Maybe in the front of the prayerbook we should print a list of all the things to look for. But Jewish services are more like an enchanted forest than a wind-up model car. Can you imagine an enchanted forest with complete instructions? What kind of adventures could you have then? Nothing surprising could ever happen.

An order The key to the entrance of the enchanted forest of Jewish services is the Hebrew word for prayerbook. It is the word *siddur*, which means "order." There is an "order" to our prayers together. You may not be aware of it because there are so many prayers. And on holy days there are more and more prayers. They seem at first as if some one just piled them up, one on top of another.

Still there is a definite order to the Jewish prayer service. It all works according to a plan, and once we learn the plan we can fit all the pieces together.

To see how the plan works, let's begin with an "order" of prayer which we know something about. If you listen to the sound of the Hebrew word *siddur*, you will hear in it the word that we use for our Pesah meal, the word *seder*. This is no accident. The word *seder*, too, means "order." And since almost all of us know about the Pesah seder, and since the seder is really a Jewish prayer service, it is a good way for us to begin to understand the Jewish idea of "order" in prayer.

One of the most wonderful things about our world is the regular way in which everything happens. We do not worry that the sun will not come up in the morning, or that the law of gravity might be repealed this afternoon. We depend upon God's creation to make sense to us. We do not expect to see a flower hanging out in the middle of space; first there must be a stem rising up out of the ground. We do not expect hens to lay chickens; first there must be an egg. If our world were not orderly, there could be no facts; and without facts, there could be no science and no religion. We could not trust God, if we could not trust His world.

We Jews believe that "order" was one of God's greatest gifts to man. We do not believe that the universe just happened; we think that God designed it very carefully. A famous rabbi, Bachya ibn Pakuda, explained how we came to believe that the world has an order with this story:

If you accidentally spilled a bottle of ink on a piece of paper, do you think that the ink would form words and that the words would spill into sentences and that the sentences would make ideas and that the ideas would tell a story? Of course not.

Yet, everything in the world tells a story; everything is made up of parts carefully put together; every part is made up of atoms. Could this all be an accident? No. The Lord who created our world made it so that we could see His plan in it. He gave the world order.

Unless we can understand our prayers, we cannot say them with true kavannah. And so, to help us understand the prayer service, the rabbis gave us an order of prayer, just as they had given us the formula of the berachah to help us to form our prayers in a simple way. It is easy to see the order in a Pesaḥ Haggadah because the Haggadah comes with a set of instructions!

At the beginning of the printed Haggadah is a list of all the things that we will do and the order in which we will do them. But does the Haggadah's order of things make sense? Let's see.

ORDER IN ALL THINGS
God's universe is orderly, governed by laws we can learn to understand. We are glad there are moral laws too, laws that show us how to act toward one another.

It would be silly to tell the story of Passover first, and then ask the Four Questions, because the answer to the Four Questions is the story. It would be silly for us to eat the meal first and then to wash our hands, for the reason we wash our hands is to clean them before we eat. It would be silly for us to say the Birkat ha-Mazon before we eat, because the Birkat ha-Mazon is the prayer thanking God for the meal which we have already eaten. And it would be silly for us to eat the Afikoman before the meal began, for the Afikoman is the piece of matzah we use to end the Pesah feast. In order to have our celebration make sense, we use the order that makes sense to us. When all the pieces are in order, they tell the story we want to tell.

Fitting the pieces together

While we are studying the Pesah seder, we should see if there are other ideas about prayer that we can find. Besides the importance of order, which is the main prayer idea in the Pesah celebration, two other ideas are also important to our study.

Two other lessons

The second idea we can see in the Pesah seder is that we Jews enjoy praying together. When we pray at the seder table, we are celebrating together with the whole Jewish people. In the Haggadah this idea is found when we are asked to imagine that *we* are the ones who were set free from slavery. And in a very real way, we are the same people, for we are still Jews and we still remember the same events that our ancestors have always remembered.

We will soon see that our prayer service calls us again and again to remember that we were slaves in Egypt, and that God freed us and gave us His laws of life. Now, as long as we follow the laws of God, we cannot be slaves to any man. Prayer helps us to remember that we are not alone, it brings us close to all Jews who are praying now and all Jews who have ever prayed.

A third lesson that we find in the Pesaḥ seder is that prayer is empty unless we join in doing something to help God bring our prayer into the world of men. One of the reasons that we Jews find the seder so delightful is that along with our prayers and our blessings, we actually do something.

We eat the matzah together to remind ourselves
of the days when we lived in poverty and slavery.
The bitter taste of the horseradish reminds us of the
bitterness of a life in bondage, and the sweet wine
tells us of the sweetness of serving the Lord. The
parsley and the saltwater remind us of God's creation,
which is all around us. And, together, as a family
and as a people, we study and teach over again the
story of our exodus from Egypt and the miracle of
freedom.

LESSONS FROM THE HAGGADAH
Order and togetherness mark the Pesaḥ seder.
Together we relive, in order, the bitterness
of bondage, the gladness of coming out of Egypt,
the sweetness of service to God.

Celebrating our Judaism

We all love the Pesaḥ seder because it is a true celebration. It is filled with song, with food and drink, with story and prayer, with memories and hopes, and with the people we love. That is why talking about the seder is such a good way to begin putting together the things we know about prayer.

Every prayer service is a celebration for the person who knows how to pray and understands prayer. Every prayer service is a celebration of the wonderful world in which we live, of the noble and beautiful ways in which people can live, of the feeling of sharing that makes us so much bigger than ourselves, of the love that passes between man and God to give us energy and peace, and of the way the world will be when all men live together as one.

Now that we have seen the order of the Pesaḥ seder and how it helps us to understand and celebrate together the story of our freedom from Egyptian slavery, we can turn to the daily prayer service and see how it helps us to celebrate together our Jewish way of life.

15

An order of prayer: Step one

t happened once in a small Polish town that all the people were invited to a great dance and celebration in the town hall. Now on the evening of the dance, a young boy who lived outside of town had come to visit friends, but could not find them at home. Indeed, he could find no one at home in the whole town.

While he was searching for the people, and thinking how strange it was that the town was empty, he chanced to walk by the town hall. Looking in through one of the windows the boy could plainly see that the entire town had gone crazy. People were jumping up and down, hugging one another, pressing one another, pushing and pulling at one another, bowing and raising their hands to one another.

Just as he was about to run away from this town full of madmen, one of the people in the town hall opened a window to let in some fresh air. It was then that the boy heard music pouring out of the hall and it was then that he understood that all the people inside were dancing.

We are sometimes like the boy at the window when we come to a prayer service. At first we cannot understand what the people are doing. They seem to know so well exactly what to do and when, and we cannot follow along very well at all. Here let us try to see how the service works by dividing it into steps. But before we do that, we should ask the question, why pray every day?

Daily prayer At first, Jews did not have daily prayer services. Instead there were daily sacrifices at the ancient Temple. In the morning and the evening, religious Jews would recite the Shema, as it was commanded. But the people learned to love praying. Praying gave them the strength they needed to face the difficult kind of life that they had to live day by day—a life of poverty and uncertainty, of hunger and need. And the prayers raised their spirits just as later, here in the United States, the spirits of the slaves were raised by the spirituals they sang and by their deep belief in God.

Even more surprising, at first the rabbis did not want to set down a daily prayer service! They really did not wish to write down any prayers for congregations to use. Perhaps they were afraid that people could not pray with kavannah while using someone else's words, someone else's prayers. And we have seen that bringing kavannah to a written prayer is one of the most difficult things about praying.

But the people won the argument and a daily prayer service was established. At first it was just the Shema and the blessings following it. But soon other prayers were added to make up the service we have now.

And, as time passed, three separate services came into being for each and every day. The morning service is called שַׁחֲרִית *Shaḥarit*, a name which comes from the Hebrew word שַׁחַר *Shaḥar*, meaning "Dawn." The short afternoon service is called מִנְחָה *Minḥah*, a name which was used for the afternoon offering to God in the Temple. (The offering was of grain and cereals.) And the last of the daily services, the evening service, is called מַעֲרִיב *Ma'ariv* or עַרְבִית *Arvit*, a name that comes from the Hebrew word עֶרֶב *Erev*, which means "Evening."

All three of the daily prayer services work in the same way, using pretty much the same steps, and

so, we will study the Shaḥarit service, which is the fullest of the daily prayer services.

The order of prayer   What is the plan of each service? The introduction is there to get us in the mood to pray. The first step in our prayer is to give thanks for the wonderful world in which we live. The second step is to give thanks that our people has been loyal to God since the time God brought us out of the land of Egypt. The third step is to ask God for the things our people needs. And the fourth step is our own private prayer, the time when each of us asks for what he wants. Then, just as there was an introduction to get us in the mood of prayer, we have a conclusion so that we can all end the service together.

There is another way to think of the steps, too. The first step tells us what God has done for us. The second step tells us what God wants us to do. The third step shows us how man and God can be partners in making a better world. And the fourth step, the silent prayer, gives us time to think how we can help and time to ask God for the kind of strength and wisdom that we will need in order to do something good in the world.

Some of our services are more complex than this. In some services we read from the Torah and add a whole special section of prayers. On the Sabbath and the Holy Days, we add an additional part to the service which we call the *Musaf*, the addition. On certain Holy Days and at the time of the New Moon, we add a special group of psalms that we call the *Hallel* service. The word *Hallel* means praise, and the Hallel service praises God.

And some services are more simple than this. The Minḥah service leaves out steps one and two because they were said just a few hours before.

But this plan will help you to understand where the service is going and what each part of the service is all about.

A rabbi was once asked, "What do you do before you pray?" And he answered, "I pray that I may be able to pray well."

When we come into the sanctuary, we are not always ready to pray. Our mind may be far away. We may be daydreaming or thinking of a problem we have, or we may be wondering what we will do when the service is over.

We have to get into the proper mood to pray, we have to bring our mind to thoughts of God and of our people. So, before we pray, we pray. That is, before the prayer service really begins, we say some psalms, or sing an opening hymn, or say a few blessings praising God. In the traditional Shaḥarit service, there is a whole section of berachot which gets us into the mood of prayer. We call this section *Birkot ha-Shaḥar*, the Morning Blessings.

PREPARING TO PRAY
How do we get in the mood to pray?
Through psalms or hymns or blessings,
or perhaps through studying a little.

Originally the Birkot ha-Shaḥar were prayers spoken at home. And, if you read them now, you can see that they follow all the actions that we take as we get up in the morning. There are blessings about getting up, getting dressed, and preparing for the new day. The first of these is the blessing for washing your hands:

> *We praise You, O Lord our God, King of the universe, who make us holy by Your commandments and command us on the washing of hands.*

There is even a small section of the Mishnah for us to study first thing in the morning. For how could a truly Jewish day begin without a little study? One thing we ask of God in Birkot ha-Shaḥar is that God make our studying a pleasure for us:

> *Please make the words of Your Torah in our mouth, and in the mouth of Your people, pleasant, O Lord our God, so that we and our children and the children of Your people, the house of Israel, may all know Your Name and study Your Torah. We praise You, O Lord, who teach the Torah to Your people Israel.*

The Birkot ha-Shaḥar bring our minds to thoughts of God through the praise and the thanks that we offer. So they have become a kind of introduction to the Shaḥarit service and in traditional synagogues, everyone says these prayers together. But, in Reform synagogues, the Birkot ha-Shaḥar have been shortened and the introduction is usually silent meditation as the congregation gathers, and then an opening hymn or psalm.

The main service really begins when the leader calls out to the congregation:

בָּרְכוּ אֶת־יְיָ הַמְבֹרָךְ׃

Give praise to the Lord to whom all praise belongs.

בָּרוּךְ יְיָ הַמְבֹרָךְ לְעוֹלָם וָעֶד׃

We praise the Lord to whom all praise belongs for ever and ever.

Because the *Borchu* is a signal for us to begin praying together, we do not usually say this prayer when we are alone or if we are praying with less than a minyan.

The call to prayer

Now that we have officially started, what should we say first? How should we begin? The best way is to begin by thanking God for the wonderful gift which He has already given us, His universe and His creation. Here are some key sentences from the morning prayer, that show how we begin:

בָּרוּךְ אַתָּה יְיָ, אֱלֹהֵינוּ מֶלֶךְ הָעוֹלָם.
יוֹצֵר אוֹר וּבוֹרֵא חֹשֶׁךְ. עֹשֶׂה שָׁלוֹם וּבוֹרֵא אֶת־הַכֹּל׃

We praise You, O Lord our God, King of the universe, Maker of light and Creator of darkness, Author of peace and Creator of all things.
In Your mercy You give light to the earth and to all who dwell upon it, and in Your goodness, You renew the work of creation continually, day by day. We praise You, O Lord, Creator of light.

The first step—God's wonderful world

We begin by thanking God for the world all around us, the universe in which we live. Through the beauty of His creation, we come to know God better.

Imagine that we were walking down a quiet road and noticed a watch on the ground. We picked it up, but as we had never seen a watch before, it was a mystery to us. At first, the gold back and the white face with its small black figures and its two black hands made us think how pretty it was, and how nice it was that someone had thought of making it. But then we began to hear it ticking, so we opened it up to take a look inside to see where the noise was coming from. Then we beheld a complex of gears and wheels whirring and turning, moving in steady patterns before our eyes. And we wondered, "How does it all work?" So we looked deeper into it, using magnifying glasses and microscopes. And we began to understand how it works, and we began to see that the one who had created the watch must have been very wise and very learned.

In the same way, we discovered our world. At first, we saw only the way things look: we came to love the trees and the flowers, the waters flowing down to the oceans, the great mountains and the mighty thunderclouds. But then, we began to look deeper into these things and found that they were even more wonderful on the inside! We still do not understand exactly how everything operates, what makes the world go on being the way it is, but we keep studying and experimenting. In the meantime we can easily see that the Creator of this world was far wiser than the wisest man, for God Himself is the greatest of all mysteries.

When we study God's world, we are trying to find the laws that God has created. We are trying to understand why things happen in the way that they do. People who devote themselves to this kind of study are called scientists.

We thank God for the light in the morning, just as we thank Him for the darkness that gives us rest in the evenings. We always start our prayers this way because if it were not a good world, then no prayers would help us. So every time we say the service, this first step helps us to recall how precious our world is. That helps us think twice before we do anything that might destroy or harm it. If the Jewish services did no more to help the world than just that, they would still be worthwhile! But that is only Step one.

OUR CHERISHED WORLD
We thank God for the beauty of the world around us. We cherish the earth. We would do nothing to harm it, but help keep it beautiful and fruitful.

16

An order of prayer:
Step two

Step two is longer and more complicated. It centers around the Shema. There is a prayer before the Shema, and after it there are some verses from the Bible, a pledge and the *Mi Chamocha*. All of the parts in this step speak of love. In Hebrew, Step two actually begins with the word *Ahavah*, which means love.

These are a few lines from the prayer *Ahavah Rabbah*, the first prayer in Step two:

אַהֲבָה רַבָּה אֲהַבְתָּנוּ יְיָ אֱלֹהֵינוּ.

Lord our God, You have shown us great love and unfailing mercy. Our fathers trusted in You and You taught them the laws of life. May we too trust in You, and learn to understand and love Your Torah.

בָּרוּךְ אַתָּה יְיָ.
הַבּוֹחֵר בְּעַמוֹ יִשְׂרָאֵל בְּאַהֲבָה:

We praise You, O Lord, who in love have called Your people Israel to serve You.

We Jews believe that God loves human beings, and cares about what happens to us. And we believe that God has shown us His love by giving us laws. In Step one, we saw that God's whole universe works by laws that we can learn through our senses. Now we can see that God's laws can teach us how we should behave, too!

God has inspired men to write about and to study the best ways of living. When we Jews study the Torah and the words, thoughts, and actions of our great teachers, we begin to understand how the world of man fits into the world of God. In a way, we are scientists looking for better ways to live, ways which make for peace and love, for justice and mercy.

Our Bible tells us that we are all created "in the image of God." And we Jews have come to understand that this means that all men should live together as one, just as God is One God. The Shema reminds us that the God who created all people is One, and so all people are brothers and sisters, all children of the same Father.

שְׁמַע יִשְׂרָאֵל יְהֹוָה אֱלֹהֵינוּ יְהֹוָה אֶחָד:

Hear, O Israel, the Lord is our God, the Lord is One.

בָּרוּךְ שֵׁם כְּבוֹד מַלְכוּתוֹ לְעוֹלָם וָעֶד:

*We praise His name whose glorious kingdom is for
ever and ever.*

THE MEANING OF THE SHEMA
The Shema reminds us that God is One.
All of us are children of the One God.
Because we are made "in His image and
likeness," we can live peaceably together.

God's love for us Now if we are to carry on the Jewish promise to serve God, what must we do? We must show our love for God. In His love, God has given us commandments and laws to follow. To show our love, we must follow them. We remind ourselves by speaking words from the Torah. The most important of these instructions is the first paragraph. Again its first word is the Hebrew word for love.

וְאָהַבְתָּ אֵת יְהֹוָה אֱלֹהֶיךָ בְּכָל־לְבָבְךָ וּבְכָל־נַפְשְׁךָ וּבְכָל־
מְאֹדֶךָ: וְהָיוּ הַדְּבָרִים הָאֵלֶּה אֲשֶׁר אָנֹכִי מְצַוְּךָ הַיּוֹם עַל־
לְבָבֶךָ: וְשִׁנַּנְתָּם לְבָנֶיךָ וְדִבַּרְתָּ בָּם בְּשִׁבְתְּךָ בְּבֵיתֶךָ וּבְלֶכְתְּךָ
בַדֶּרֶךְ וּבְשָׁכְבְּךָ וּבְקוּמֶךָ: וּקְשַׁרְתָּם לְאוֹת עַל־יָדֶךָ וְהָיוּ
לְטֹטָפֹת בֵּין עֵינֶיךָ: וּכְתַבְתָּם עַל־מְזֻזוֹת בֵּיתֶךָ וּבִשְׁעָרֶיךָ:

And you shall love the Lord your God with all your heart, with all your soul and with all your might.
And these words which I command you this day shall be upon your heart; and you shall teach them diligently to your children, and you shall talk of them when you sit in your house, when you walk by the way, and when you lie down, and when you rise up. And you shall bind them as a sign upon your hand, and they shall be like frontlets between your eyes. And you shall write them on the doorposts of your house, and upon your gates.

Loving and obeying God Keeping this promise is the heart of being a Jew. That is what our people has been trying to do wherever Jews have lived throughout the centuries. We are reminded of this each time we recite the Shema. And we are still trying to keep our promise today.

The last two parts of the second step are about this. First we repeat that we still believe that we should obey God's laws and commandments:

True it is that You are first and You are last,
And besides You we have no king . . .

We even give an example showing how we know that God loves Israel:

You, O Lord our God, brought us out of Egypt and freed
us from the house of slavery . . .

Then, we learn that one of the ways in which we Jews have always thanked God is through our prayers. For as soon as the people of Israel were free from slavery, we realized that God had truly helped us. We even remember the words which we said:

Thanking God for His help

מִי־כָמֹכָה בָּאֵלִם יְיָ.
מִי כָּמֹכָה נֶאְדָּר בַּקֹּדֶשׁ.
נוֹרָא תְהִלֹּת. עֹשֵׂה־פֶלֶא:

Who is like You, O Lord, among the gods men worship? Who
is like You, majestic in splendor, doing wonders?

יְיָ יִמְלֹךְ לְעֹלָם וָעֶד:

The Lord shall reign for ever and ever!

Now we can see where Step two has taken us. Our fathers were slaves, but they trusted in God and he brought them out of Egypt. In return they promised to serve God forever. And that is what we say today. In the morning our second step comes to an end when we ask God to save Jews who are in trouble, and in the evening when we ask God to care for all of us.

So far, in steps one and two, our service has talked about three very important Jewish ideas. First, we said that God is the creator of the world and that He creates it day by day. Second, we said that God loves us and cares about us, and shows us His love by giving us the laws of life. We show our love for God by trying to follow His laws. The third idea is that when we obey God's laws and serve God, then God helps us by making us free, just as He did when we were slaves in Egypt and He brought us out of Egypt.

God's people Israel Our people, Israel, is a good example of how God's laws work. Even though we are spread all over the world, we still believe that we are one people serving One God; and so we have been able to stay alive through all the centuries while stronger nations have come and gone. Where the Shema is written in the Torah scroll, it looks like this:

שְׁמַע יִשְׂרָאֵל יהוה אֱלֹהֵינוּ יהוה אֶחָד

Why are there two letters so much larger than the rest? The rabbis explained that these two letters together make the Hebrew word עֵד *Ed*, which means witness. Here in the Shema, which talks to Israel, the people of Israel are asked to be a witness — to show the rest of the world that we can all be free together, if we will only follow the laws of God.

HIS WITNESSES
The people of Israel are witnesses
to the Oneness and goodness of God.
We know that we can live in freedom
by following God's laws.

17

An order of prayer: Step three

 The third step has a name. It is called the *Amidah*, which means the "standing" prayer; or the *Tefillah*, the "Prayer." In the morning daily service it has nineteen berachot; on the Sabbath is has only seven, and on other holy days the number and the parts change.

Step three— Tefillah
What does not change is what is happening in this step. It is here in the third step that we ask God to provide help for the people of Israel and for our congregation and ourselves. In the first step we talked to God as the Maker and Lawgiver of the whole universe. In the second step we spoke to God as the God of Israel. Now we will speak to God, our Helper and Guide, our Partner.

So we begin by recalling God's close ties with our forefathers, Abraham, Isaac, and Jacob.

142

בָּרוּךְ אַתָּה יְיָ. אֱלֹהֵינוּ וֵאלֹהֵי אֲבוֹתֵינוּ.
אֱלֹהֵי אַבְרָהָם. אֱלֹהֵי יִצְחָק. וֵאלֹהֵי יַעֲקֹב.

We praise You, O Lord our God and God of our fathers, God of Abraham, God of Isaac and God of Jacob . . . You remember the faithfulness of our fathers . . . Kingly Helper, Savior and Shield . . .

We know how God helped our forefathers; how God cared for Abraham in all the years that Abraham wandered; how God protected Isaac from being sacrificed; how Jacob was saved from the hand of Esau, his brother. And now, we hope that God will help us, too. **Prayer for help**

In the next berachah, we ask God to help us now. To help us in our daily life, by giving us His love. We can see how God helps us day by day. And we believe that even when we die God does not forget us.

We also remind ourselves that God is holy. At first, you may think this is a strange place for us to stop and say, "You are holy, and Your name is holy . . . ." Really, it is a very good place.

We are about to ask God for things that we want, things that we think we need. This is a good place to remind ourselves that we are talking to the God who rules all things. We must not be selfish in our wants.

Now we come to the heart of the Tefillah. With thirteen berachot we ask God for all we need. **The thirteen central blessings**

The first six of the thirteen are for personal things: we ask for the gifts of wisdom, for God's forgiveness when we do wrong, for understanding so that we know when we have done something wrong, for God's help when we are in trouble, for God's help in freeing us from illness, and for God's help in freeing us from poverty and want.

Then follow six blessings for our people: we ask for the regathering of the people Israel from all the corners of the earth, for good leaders to make our people strong and wise, for protection from those who would harm us and from our own mistakes, for God's help to be given to those who deserve it, for the rebuilding of Israel, and for the coming of the days of the Messiah.

Finally we add a blessing asking God to hear all our prayers and to answer all our needs by helping us. Like the other berachot in the Amidah, this one is very short. Here is the whole prayer:

Hear our voice,
O Lord our God;
Save us and have mercy on us,
Accept our prayers
With mercy and favor
For You are a God
Who listens to prayers
And hears our needs.
From Your presence,
O King,
Do not let us go away
Empty-handed
For You listen in mercy
To the prayers of Your people,
Israel.
We praise You, O Lord,
Who hear prayer.

There is a tradition that after the words "Empty-handed" we can ask God for anything we want, anything that is on our mind; and we can ask God for help for ourselves, for our family or for our neighbors. Even though we have a special place in the prayer service set aside for our private prayers, this place helps to make the service more personal for us.

Together these thirteen benedictions are the heart of the Amidah. By studying them, we can see the things that Jews have found to be important. There is no prayer for God to make us rich. There is no prayer for God to do our work for us. And there is no selfish prayer.

We do not have room in this book to look closely at each of the thirteen central benedictions of the Amidah, but we will look at one of the personal ones and one of the blessings for our people.

Prayer for forgiveness

We all make mistakes, but our rabbis have taught us that inside each of our mistakes is the chance for us to do better. We must ask for forgiveness and then try to do the right thing. Each day we turn to God and ask His forgiveness for any sin that we may have committed.

סְלַח־לָנוּ אָבִינוּ כִּי חָטָאנוּ. מְחַל־לָנוּ מַלְכֵּנוּ כִּי פָשָׁעְנוּ. כִּי מוֹחֵל וְסוֹלֵחַ אָתָּה. בָּרוּךְ אַתָּה יְיָ. חַנּוּן הַמַּרְבֶּה לִסְלוֹחַ:

Forgive us, our Father, for we have sinned;
pardon us, our King, for we have transgressed;
for You are eager to pardon and forgive.
We praise You, O gracious Lord, abundant in
forgiveness.

But, you may ask, why should I ask God for forgiveness if I have not sinned? The answer is in the prayer. Even though you may not have sinned, we are praying together as a congregation, and we are praying together, too, with all Israel. If just one man has sinned, we all should help by asking for God to forgive him.

There is another idea in this prayer, too. We say that God is "eager" to forgive us. We Jews believe that God loves the man who turns away from sin and asks for forgiveness. Our tradition teaches that it is worse to sin against another person than to sin against God. When we sin against another person, that person may move away and we may never be able to ask forgiveness. But the Lord is everywhere, only waiting for us to turn to Him.

I'M SORRY
If we make a mistake we try to learn from it, and do better. If we have wronged anyone, we ask him to forgive us. We ask God to forgive us too.

Two of the prayers for our people should catch your eye. One is the prayer for God to gather up Israel from the four corners of the world and bring the people together again as in the days of old. And so He has done! After repeating this prayer day after day for two thousand years, the Jews have come to see the day in which the prayer was to be answered. The modern state of Israel is truly a sign of hope for us, for if God has answered this prayer than we can hope He will answer other prayers of our people, too.

Of course, the answer would be lost if we did not remember God's help, and so we pray that God will return with us to Jerusalem, to dwell with His people.

וְלִירוּשָׁלַיִם עִירְךָ בְּרַחֲמִים תָּשׁוּב.
בָּרוּךְ אַתָּה יְיָ. בּוֹנֵה יְרוּשָׁלָיִם:

And to Jerusalem, Your city, return in mercy, and dwell there as You have promised. Rebuild it soon in our days as an everlasting homeland, and speedily set up in it the throne of David. We praise You, O Lord, Builder of Jerusalem.

Along with the hope that God would help us to rebuild our homeland, we Jews have always hoped that we would remember God and live according to His laws after our homeland was rebuilt. So, too, today. We hope that the people of Israel will act in the spirit of God's laws, so that other nations will see that it is good to live according to God's commandments.

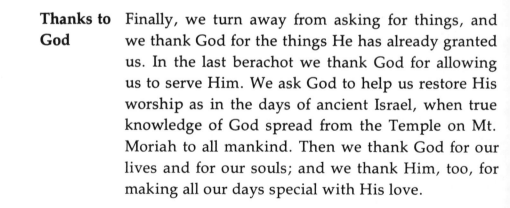

THE RETURN

Many Jews returned to the homeland when the State of Israel was reborn in modern times. Now we pray that the spirit of God will dwell in Israel; that His law go forth from Zion to the world.

Thanks to God

Finally, we turn away from asking for things, and we thank God for the things He has already granted us. In the last berachot we thank God for allowing us to serve Him. We ask God to help us restore His worship as in the days of ancient Israel, when true knowledge of God spread from the Temple on Mt. Moriah to all mankind. Then we thank God for our lives and for our souls; and we thank Him, too, for making all our days special with His love.

Prayer for peace

Perhaps you can see where all these blessings have led us. The last berachah of the Amidah is the prayer for peace.

שִׂים שָׁלוֹם. טוֹבָה וּבְרָכָה. חֵן וָחֶסֶד וְרַחֲמִים.
עָלֵינוּ וְעַל־כָּל־יִשְׂרָאֵל עַמֶּךְ:
בָּרוּךְ אַתָּה יְיָ. הַמְבָרֵךְ אֶת־עַמּוֹ יִשְׂרָאֵל בַּשָּׁלוֹם:

Grant peace, welfare and blessing, grace and love and mercy,
to us; to all Israel, Your people. Bless us, our Father, all
of us together, with the light of Your attention, for by Your
light You have shown us, O Lord our God, the Law of life,
a love of kindness and righteousness, blessing and mercy, life
and peace.
For it is good in Your sight that mankind be blessed with
enduring peace.
We praise You, O Lord, who bless Your people Israel with
peace.

No other blessing is quite as precious to us as the berachah for peace. All of us understand that this is God's most precious gift. Our most difficult task is to bring peace into the world around us. Still, God has given us the knowledge of what peace is like. He has created peace in the heavens and perfect peace in our hearts. We must learn to act in such a way that we will bring that peace into our everyday lives.

Changes in the Amidah

In traditional synagogues, the Amidah is said twice. Once, the members of the congregation stand reading the Amidah to themselves quietly. Then the nineteen berachot are repeated aloud by the reader or the cantor. When we read the Amidah aloud, we make a few changes in it. And on the Sabbath and Holy Days we change it, too. But by repeating it over and over, we come to understand how the partnership between man and God works; we learn what kind of help we can hope for from God and what we must do for ourselves.

18

An order of prayer:
Step four

In traditional communities, when a man came to the fourth step, the silent prayer, he would raise his *tallit* over his head and enclose himself in it completely. He was making a small private place where he could say his personal prayer to God.

Being alone with God The fourth step in our prayer service is the time when you must look inside of yourself and ask God for the things *you* want.

From the world, to the Jews, to the people of your congregation, we now come to you. Our prayer circle has got smaller and smaller. We have said together the things we needed to say. Now it is your turn.

It need not be a long prayer. You do not even have to say any words. It may just be a prayer in your heart, a feeling or a thought. That is how personal it is supposed to be.

Sometimes, though, we cannot find a prayer in our hearts. We are embarrassed or shy, or our thoughts are confused. For times when we cannot think of any prayer of our own, the rabbis have given us a private prayer that we may say instead. It is the personal prayer of a fourth-century rabbi, Mar the son of Ravina, and we find it in the Talmud:

אֱלֹהַי. נְצֹר לְשׁוֹנִי מֵרָע. וּשְׂפָתַי מִדַּבֵּר מִרְמָה:

O my God!
Guard my tongue from evil
And my lips from speaking falsely.

יִהְיוּ לְרָצוֹן אִמְרֵי־פִי. וְהֶגְיוֹן לִבִּי לְפָנֶיךָ. יְיָ צוּרִי וְגֹאֲלִי:

Let the words of my mouth
And the meditation of my heart
Be acceptable to You, O Lord,
My Rock and my Redeemer.

Other private prayers have been recorded in Jewish prayerbooks, but this is the one most often used. it is the only prayer in the Amidah, which talks of "me" instead of "we."

After all the things you've had to think about in the first three steps, will you be selfish and ask for a new bicycle or a new sweater?

Or will the Jewish service have changed you a little? Coming into the synagogue our thoughts are filled with "me." My problems, my needs, my wants. Now we have spent some time together with God, thinking about His world and what He wants of people. If

What do you think the Psalmist means
when he speaks of "the secret place
of the Most High"? Consider again
the prayer of Rabbi Mar.

we have been praying with kavannah, we have
changed a little.

**Partners
with God** Now that we have heard the service, we know that
we are not alone in the world. We are part of a marvelous community and God is our partner. As one rabbi
told us, "God is high above the world! Yet if a man
enters a synagogue and hides behind a post and prays
in a tiny whisper, the Holy One, blessed be He, listens to the prayer. . . . Can there be a God nearer
than this, who is as near to His creatures as the mouth
is to the ear?"

God is listening, what will you say?
God is with you, what will you do?

We add some prayers after this to bring the service
to an end. We will talk about them in Chapter 22.
But when you learn to become a new person, a true
Jew, each time you say the prayer service, then you
have already got the point of Jewish prayer. That
is why we have given our service an order.

19

Prayer and study

People of many different religions use the kinds of prayers that we have spoken of. All people who pray ask for help, praise God for His gifts, and try to come closer to God through their prayers. There are Christian sects that try to reach God as the Jewish Ḥasidim do, through song and dance, through joy and rejoicing. Just as there is a Ḥasidic story about a Ḥasid who laughed and laughed and laughed trying to come closer to God through his laughter, so there is a story of a Zen Buddhist master who tried the very same trick!

All the prayers of which we have spoken, including the berachot, which praise and thank God for His wonders, and for His commandments, are like ways that other men have used to come closer to understanding God. They are ways of reaching out from

our place, here in the world, to God's place within and around us.

One of our great rabbis, Rav Kook, has taught us that the Jews have another way of praying—a special Jewish way of prayer. He said that there are two main parts of the siddur. The first part is made up of prayers that come from below and are lifted high into the heavens. The second part of the siddur is made up of the Torah. Through the Torah we try to bring God's love into our world.

The teachings of the Torah are like seeds. When we plant them in ourselves, they grow and fill us with life. To plant them we must study; and, in Judaism, study can be prayer.

EARTH AND HEAVEN
Our prayers go up to God.
And as we bring
the Torah down into our lives,
more and more of God's
love comes to us.

Study is so important to Jewish prayer that the greatest of all Jewish prayers, the Shema, is a "prayer of study." When the rabbis who were writing the Mishnah began to consider prayer, they started with the question: "From what time may Shema be read in the evenings?" The man who wrote this question already knew that he had to say the Shema.

When you lie down and when you rise up

The commandment to say the Shema is found right in the paragraph after the Shema itself. There it says: "and you shall talk of [these words] when you sit in your house, when you walk by the way; when you lie down and when you rise up." In other words, Jews were asked to pray the Shema at least twice a day—when we rise and when we lie down.

But the Shema is a strange kind of prayer. It does not ask for anything. It is not a prayer thanking God for anything. It is not even addressed to God. Instead of speaking to God, the Shema prayer speaks to the person who is praying and to all Israel. Still the Shema prayer is the most important Jewish prayer.

And we have already studied the reason! The Shema is the best example of a prayer that brings the life of the Torah into our everyday world. Within the three paragraphs are laws that command us to say prayers, to love God, to follow God's laws, to dedicate our lives to God's service, to dedicate our homes to God through the mezuzah, and to teach our children the laws of God.

Ever since the time of the Romans, Jews have been called the "People of the Book," *Am ha-Sefer*. In order to make the Jews forget their religion, the Romans

The People of the Book

ordered us to stop studying and teaching the Torah. When Rabbi Akiba heard the new Roman law, he told this story:

A hungry fox once came to the edge of a stream and seeing a school of fish swimming in the center of the stream, decided that he would trick one of the fish and then catch it for his supper. He called to an old and large grandfather fish, "Come over here, I have an important thing to tell you."

The grandfather fish came swimming near the fox, keeping just out of the fox's reach. "What is it?" he asked.

The fox smiled and said, "A fisherman is coming this way. He will catch you and eat you for his supper if you do not escape quickly." The fox paused to lick his shiny fur, then continued, "If you will come out of the water, I will take you downstream far from the fisherman's net."

"No thank you," said the old grandfather fish. "In the water, I can swim and perhaps escape the net, but out of the water I have no protection, and I will surely die." He swam away from the hungry fox.

So you see, Akiba said, as long as the Jewish people continue to study the Torah, they may still live; but the Jewish people without the Torah is like a fish without water, and they will surely perish.

We Jews believe that it is important for every Jew to know and understand the words of the Torah. And one of our prayers echoes the story of Rabbi Akiba when it says that the Torah's words are "our life and the length of our days, and we should study them day and night."

In order to do this, to study the words of the law day and night, passages from the Torah are a part of the regular prayer service. The Priestly Blessing, the blessing first pronounced by Aaron, Moses' brother, is included in the morning service so that we can follow the commandment to study the Torah each day. You probably know this blessing very well. Here it is:

יְבָרֶכְךָ יְיָ וְיִשְׁמְרֶךָ:

The Lord bless you and guard you.

יָאֵר יְיָ פָּנָיו אֵלֶיךָ וִיחֻנֶּךָ:

The Lord cause His light to shine upon you and be gracious unto you.

יִשָּׂא יְיָ פָּנָיו אֵלֶיךָ. וְיָשֵׂם לְךָ שָׁלוֹם:

The Lord look with favor upon you and give you peace.

Other parts of the Torah, and some parts of the Talmud, are also in the prayer service so that we may study them. To remind us of the ancient Temple, where animals were sacrificed, we still recite the laws of sacrificing animals on weekdays and on holidays. Even though these laws are a part of the regular prayer service, we can not really call them prayer unless we understand that studying is really a kind of praying.

And of course the most important kind of prayer-study is the reading from the Torah itself. A whole special addition to the prayer service is used whenever we read from the scroll of the Torah. We say special blessings before and after reading from the Torah, and recite special prayers while we are removing the scroll from the Aron Kodesh, the Holy Ark; and when we are replacing it in the Ark.

In the blessing that we use before reading from the Torah, we can see why the study of the Torah is so important to us as Jews:

בָּרְכוּ אֶת־יְיָ הַמְבֹרָךְ:

Praise the Lord to whom all praise is due.

בָּרוּךְ יְיָ הַמְבֹרָךְ לְעוֹלָם וָעֶד:

Praise the Lord to whom all praise is due for ever and ever.

בָּרוּךְ אַתָּה יְיָ. אֱלֹהֵינוּ מֶלֶךְ הָעוֹלָם. אֲשֶׁר בָּחַר־בָּנוּ מִכָּל־ הָעַמִּים. וְנָתַן־לָנוּ אֶת־תּוֹרָתוֹ. בָּרוּךְ אַתָּה יְיָ. נוֹתֵן הַתּוֹרָה:

We praise You, O Lord our God, King of the universe, who chose us from among all peoples to reveal to us Your Torah. We praise You, O Lord, Giver of the Torah.

Prayer helps us to become the kind of person who wants to do something to help the world. Jewish prayer teaches us to be unselfish, to think of the needs and wants of others, and to try to live at peace with nature. But without study we cannot know *what* we can do to make our world a better place in which to live. Only through study do we come to know what God requires of us; what we can do.

Just as a scientist devotes his life to studying the way in which the world works, the laws that help us to learn more about the way in which the universe is bound together, the Jew studies the laws of a good life. For centuries we Jews have discussed, observed, and taught the best ways for human beings to behave,

LIVING AND LEARNING

It is important to discover the laws that govern our world. It is important, too, to seek out the moral laws that govern us in accordance with God's word.

the ways for us to make the world a pleasant and peaceful place in which we can all live together happily as members of one family. These two kinds of laws—the laws of the world around us and the laws of the world within us—are both important to us.

Study and kavannah

We have already seen that prayer without kavannah is really not prayer at all, but just the speaking of words. But what kind of kavannah can we bring to our study? The word *study* means that we need to learn something. Can we truly have kavannah while we are trying to learn?

One rabbi explained by this answer: When a person gives all of himself to the study of the Torah and mitzvot, he draws near to God and the world of God becomes a part of him. Then, when that person rises to pray, he will find it easy to pray with kavannah. Because of the way in which the person studied, God will already be in that person's heart.

20

Actions to fit our words

Over the years we have found that it helps us to put kavannah in our prayers if we use our whole bodies, as well as our thoughts. Many Jews will move their bodies back and forth as they pray, swaying even while they are sitting down. We call this swaying "shukling," a word that comes to us from the Yiddish language.

You may find it easier to pray if you use some of these actions, so we will give you a few to try. We cannot list all the actions that Jews have used in this small space, but we will give you some that are popular among the Jews of Europe and the United States.

To help you concentrate with all your might when you say the Shema prayer, you can hold your hands over your eyes and close them tightly. That way, you can concentrate on "hearing" the Shema. Another thing that we can do with the Shema is to stretch out the word Eḥad, which means "One," when we say it. We do this to remind us of all the wonderful ideas which we Jews have found in this idea that God is One.

During the Amidah, traditional Jews bend their knees as they say the first two blessings and the one that is next-to-last. They also bow from the waist as they say the prayer that begins with *Modim,* which means "Thanks." By bending the knee and bowing, we show that we look up to God as our King, and also that no matter what God's answer may be, we will accept that answer as a man accepts the word of a king. You can try these actions, too.

Bowing and bending the knee

During the *Aleinu* or Adoration, of course, we all bend our knees and bow our heads to show that God is our King and we will obey His laws.

According to different customs, Jews have many different kinds of actions that we can use to help us while we pray. When, in the Tefillah, we ask God's forgiveness for anything that we might have done that was wrong, we can follow the ancient custom of beating our hearts with the right hand to show that we really mean what we are saying from the very depths of our heart.

Other customs

Some Jews, as they are beginning the Tefillah, take a few steps forward, as if they were entering the Kingdom of Heaven to plead before the holy King. Then, at the end of the Tefillah, they take a few steps

Actions to fit our words   161

backward, to show that they are stepping out of the heavenly court.

Using the tallit and tefillin

טַלִּית
תְּפִלִּין

צִיצִית

Traditional Jews, who wear the tallit on the Shabbat and festivals, and who wear the tallit and tefillin during their daily prayers each morning, have many actions that concern these prayer helps. For example, when they come to the commandment for wearing the tefillin on the forehead, they touch the tefillin box with their fingers and then kiss their fingers, and when they read the commandment for the tefillin on the arm, they do the same with the box they are wearing on their arm. The kissing reminds them that they are doing the commandment of God, in the same way that we touch our fingers to a mezuzah as we come in and go out of our house to remind us that we should do all God's laws as we sit in our house and as we walk by the way.

As they read the commandments in the Shema for the fringes of the tallit (called *Tsitsit*), the traditional Jews gather up the fringes of their own tallit and kiss the fringes. Again, they do this to remind themselves that they are obeying God's law. If you wear a tallit, you can perform this action, too.

For some Jews, praying is almost a way of dancing. Of course, the steps are small, but the idea is the same. We have already talked about one of the most beautiful steps in this "prayer/dance."

In order to make a private place, even in the middle of the congregation, the Jew in traditional communities made a kind of tent with his tallit by raising it over his head. Then he was alone, in a way, even though he was standing with his whole congregation. This beautiful custom has almost disappeared, and yet it is like a lovely step in a dance.

Sometimes individual Jews have special actions that they alone perform, but which they feel have special **Personal ways of** meaning for them. As long as these actions help them **praying** to pray and do not keep others from concentrating, then they are good. But if the actions become more important than the prayer and its meaning, then they are not good. You must see for yourself which actions are good for you.

All of these actions help to bring life into the words of the service. They help us in another way, too. The actions remind us that the prayer service is not just words written on a page. The words need to be put into actions.

In a way, all our prayers are dreams waiting to come true. God gave us the power to dream, and even the power to make our dreams come true.

21

Special services for special times

Celebrating special days calls for special services. Most of our Holy Days have poems and prayers in celebration of a holy occasion. Still, the basic four parts of the prayer service hardly change at all. We can count on them to remind us of God's wonderful creation; of our people's special covenant with God; of what we need from God so that we can help in building a world in which God's laws will be the laws of all people; and of our special, personal sense of God's nearness.

Yet, in order to make new prayer services for each special celebration, we do make changes. Sometimes the changes are very small; for example, we say a different psalm for each day of the week. And sometimes the changes are larger. There are so many additions and changes in the prayer services for the festivals and High Holy Days that we need a special prayerbook called the *Mahzor* just for these days.

Although we cannot talk about all the changes, we can see how we add or subtract prayers to make up different services. Of course, the best way to see how the changing works, is to go to services regularly. But here we can get an idea of the major changes: the Torah service, the Musaf for Sabbath and for festivals, and for the High Holy Day services. We also want to talk about the concluding prayers, the prayers we use to end our services. They, too, are a part of the design of our prayer service.

The Torah service

Really we have already spoken about the Torah service when we talked about prayer and study. Just as you would imagine, the Torah service is added after Step four, after our private prayer. In traditional synagogues, the Torah is read on Mondays and Thursdays, and in all synagogues it is read on Shabbat and on the Holy Days.

Once there were two systems for how much to read each week. In the land of Israel, they read smaller portions and so it took three years to go from one end of the Torah scroll to the other. In Babylonia, they read bigger sections each week so it took only one year to complete the reading of the Torah. Today, we Jews follow the Babylonian custom. We begin the new weekly portion in traditional synagogues at the Saturday afternoon service, as if we could not wait a full week to begin the new section. But it really is the next Sabbath's portion. In the same way, on Simhat Torah, when we complete the reading of the Sefer Torah, we begin again on the very same day.

AN ENDLESS CHAIN
On the day of Simhat Torah,
when reading of the Sefer Torah
is completed, we begin to read it again.
In traditional synagogues, the reading of the
next Sabbath's portion is begun
on Saturday afternoon

Musaf On the Shabbat and on the festivals, we celebrate by resting from work. And since we are resting, we have more time to devote to prayer. So our prayer service is somewhat longer than the daily morning service which we have already studied. For example, there are more psalms in the introduction to the service, to get us into the mood of the Holy Day we are celebrating.

מוּסָף

Each Shabbat in the ancient Temple, a special sacrifice was offered. Since it was in addition to the daily sacrifice, it was called the *Musaf*, which means "additional" sacrifice. We have never had sacrifices in our synagogues, but we remember the Musaf, and traditional Jews say an extra Tefillah on Shabbat and on the Festivals. We call this extra part the Musaf Service. And we add it after the Torah service.

Why do we substitute prayers for sacrifices? Because our sages taught us in the Talmud that God loves prayer more than sacrifice.

The Mahzor On the High Holy Days, our prayer service changes a great deal, even though it still looks the same from the outside. We still begin with the Borchu, Call to Prayer, and we still follow the four steps, we still

166   *The order of our prayers*

have psalms and prayers to help us get in the mood of the services, and we have concluding prayers that help to bring all the ideas of the prayer service together for us.

What changes most in the services for Rosh Hashanah and Yom Kippur are the *ideas* of the service. The High Holy Days are a time for us to begin our new year by looking carefully into ourselves, by asking ourselves if we are following God's laws in the best way we can, by remembering the covenant that we have made with God and trying to see if we are doing our share, and by pleading with God to help us understand what we can do in the coming year to help us grow into better persons.

Of course, the step that is most different is the third step, the Tefillah. Our needs and wants are different on these two days because we have set aside Rosh Hashanah and Yom Kippur as days of returning, of *teshuvah*. This idea of teshuvah is one of the most beautiful of all Jewish ideas. When we sin, we are turning away from God. Sometimes we do this without meaning to do it. On Rosh Hashanah and Yom Kippur, we ask God to forgive us.

We add a special part of the service for the blowing of the *shofar*, which reminds us of the help that God gave us when He brought us out of the land of Egypt so that we might forever serve God alone. And, as we listen to the sound of the shofar, we remember God's kindness; we remember that God cares about us and helps us, and that God will save us always if we will only turn to Him.

The prayer services of Rosh Hashanah and Yom Kippur are like a beautiful melody. Each of them is a note in the song. And with each new note, we are filled with new thoughts. On Rosh Hashanah eve and in the services during the day of Rosh Hashanah, we speak of God as the Judge of all the world; the shofar reminds us that it was God alone who created the universe and who gave us the laws of life.

We know that God is our King, but He is also our Father. In a serious mood, we say a prayer that calls out to God forty-four times with the words *Avinu Malkenu*. Here are some of the lines:

אָבִינוּ מַלְכֵּנוּ, אֵין לָנוּ מֶלֶךְ אֶלָּא אָתָּה:

אָבִינוּ מַלְכֵּנוּ, עֲשֵׂה עִמָּנוּ לְמַעַן שְׁמֶךָ:

אָבִינוּ מַלְכֵּנוּ, חַדֵּשׁ עָלֵינוּ שָׁנָה טוֹבָה:

Our Father, our King!
  We have no King but You.
Our Father, our King!
  Let a happy year begin for us.
Our Father, our King!
  Fill our hands with Your blessings.
Our Father, our King!
  Open the gates of heaven to our prayers.
Our Father, our King!
  Be gracious unto us and answer us,
  For we have nothing of our own.
  Handle us with loving care and mercy,
  Save us.

HIGH HOLY DAYS
On Rosh Hashanah and Yom Kippur we ask ourselves how well we have been obeying God's laws. We acknowledge God as Judge and King and Father. We ask Him for forgiveness and help in doing better.

Our melody begins to rise on the eve of Yom Kippur when the cantor chants the Kol Nidre. We are not exactly sure where this prayer was first said, but it has come to mean a great deal to us.

כָּל־נִדְרֵי וֶאֱסָרֵי וַחֲרָמֵי

וְקוֹנָמֵי וְכִנּוּיֵי וְקִנּוּסֵי

וּשְׁבוּעוֹת. דִּנְדַרְנָא

וְדִאִשְׁתַּבַּעְנָא וְדַאֲחֲרִימְנָא

וְדַאֲסַרְנָא עַל נַפְשָׁתָנָא,

מִיּוֹם כִּפּוּרִים זֶה עַד יוֹם .....

All vows, bonds, promises, obligations, and oaths which we have vowed, sworn, and bound ourselves from this Day of Atonement to the next Day of Atonement, may it be good for us; of all these we repent. They shall be erased, released, annulled, made void, and have no effect; they shall not be binding nor shall they have any power. Our vows shall not be vows; our bonds shall not be bonds; and our oaths shall not be oaths.

Of course, we are not talking about the promises that we might make to other people, we are speaking only of those we make to God, and in a way, to ourselves. We Jews know that all people make promises that they cannot keep. Sometimes people even forget the promises they have made. But God does not forget, so we ask Him to forgive us for promises that we might not keep.

In worse times, Jews were often made to bow down to earthly kings or to declare their loyalty to another religion. But when times got better, when they could again practice their Judaism in freedom, they felt bad about the oaths that they had made to other gods. The Kol Nidre prayer was their way of saying that those words did not really count in their hearts, that they only truly worshiped the Lord, the One God.

All during the day of Yom Kippur we ask God to forgive us for sins that we have committed, or for sins that were committed by any one of our people, for we are all responsible for one another. We turn to God and plead for Him to forgive us. We confess to God that we have sinned in the past year, and to make sure that we do not forget what sins we committed, we confess the many sins that men may do. In the prayer *Al Ḥet,* we ask God to forgive all of us together for all our sins:

עַל חֵטְא שֶׁחָטָאנוּ לְפָנֶיךָ בְּאֹנֶס וּבְרָצוֹן.
וְעַל חֵטְא שֶׁחָטָאנוּ לְפָנֶיךָ בִּבְלִי דָעַת:
עַל חֵטְא שֶׁחָטָאנוּ לְפָנֶיךָ בְּגִלּוּי עֲרָיוֹת.
וְעַל חֵטְא שֶׁחָטָאנוּ לְפָנֶיךָ בְּדַעַת וּבְמִרְמָה:

We have sinned against You
  Without wanting to, and also wanting to.
We have sinned against You
  By closing our minds to reason.
We have sinned against You
  By hurting others.
We have sinned against You
  By being disrespectful to parents and teachers.
We have sinned against You
  By using violence.

וְעַל כֻּלָּם אֱלוֹהַּ סְלִיחוֹת. סְלַח לָנוּ. מְחַל לָנוּ. כַּפֶּר־לָנוּ:
For all these sins, O forgiving God,
  Forgive us, pardon us, grant us atonement.

The Neilah service

The last note in the melody of the High Holy Days is the *Neilah* service, the "closing" service. Normally, the people who prayed at the ancient Temple would go home after the Minḥah sacrifice. But on Yom Kippur, they stayed until sunset, that is, right up to the time when the Temple gates were closing. In the same way, we think of the heavenly gates of forgiveness "closing" as Yom Kippur comes to an end.

We open the doors of the Aron Kodesh and the congregation stands for the entire Neilah service. The chanting and the prayers are all serious and solemn, as we ask God one last time to forgive us for our sins and to grant us a year of blessing for us and for all mankind. As the Day of Atonement closes, we recite the *piyyutim*, poems written by men who devoted themselves to asking God for His help and His forgiveness.

> *O You who hear weeping, hear our sobs.*
> *And keep our tears as treasures in Your heavenly store,*
> *Deliver us; save us from Your dread decrees,*
> *For our eyes turn to You evermore.*

Finally the Aron Kodesh is closed, and we sound the shofar again, and sing לַשָׁנָה הַבָּאָה בִּירוּשָׁלַיִם: *Lashanah ha-ba'ah b'Yerushalayim,* Next Year in Jerusalem.

22

The closing prayers

We have not yet spoken about the closing prayers of every service for two reasons. First, they are the closing prayers and so it is good to end with them, just as we always do at our prayer services. Second, the most important of the two is the Adoration, which was originally used only on Rosh Hashanah, so we wanted first to see what the Rosh Hashanah service was about.

Ever since the fourteenth century we have been using the *Aleinu*, the "Adoration," in our daily and festival services. But even so, we can hear in it the echoes of the ideas of Rosh Hashanah:

The Adoration

עָלֵינוּ לְשַׁבֵּחַ לַאֲדוֹן הַכֹּל
לָתֵת גְּדֻלָּה לְיוֹצֵר בְּרֵאשִׁית:
שֶׁלֹּא עָשָׂנוּ כְּגוֹיֵי הָאֲרָצוֹת
וְלֹא שָׂמָנוּ כְּמִשְׁפְּחוֹת הָאֲדָמָה:
שֶׁלֹּא שָׂם חֶלְקֵנוּ כָּהֶם
וְגוֹרָלֵנוּ כְּכָל־הֲמוֹנָם:

It is our duty to praise
the Lord of all things,
to tell of His greatness
who formed the world in the beginning,
for He has not made us like nations of other lands,
and He has not made us like other families of the earth,
for He has not given us a portion like theirs,
nor a fortune like all of them.

וַאֲנַחְנוּ כֹּרְעִים וּמִשְׁתַּחֲוִים וּמוֹדִים
לִפְנֵי מֶלֶךְ מַלְכֵי הַמְּלָכִים
הַקָּדוֹשׁ בָּרוּךְ הוּא:

We bend the knee and offer worship and thanks
before the supreme King of kings,
the Holy One, blessed be He,
who stretch out the heavens and establish the earth,
whose glory is in the heavens above,
and whose might is in the highest heights.
He is our God;
there is none else.

The Adoration brings together many ideas from the
service. In it we can see the idea that God rules over
the universe which He created, and that is the idea
of Step one. There is the Jewish belief in the oneness
of God, too, which is the idea of Step two, the Shema.
From Step three, the Adoration takes the idea of partnership between man and God, as we pray for God

to establish His "kingdom" in all the earth, so that all nations will see that God is One.

Originally when the congregation said the words, "We bend the knee . . ." each person lay flat on the floor; but as time passed a different custom arose. Now many Jews bend their knees at the word כֹּרְעִים and bow a little at the word וּמִשְׁתַּחֲוִים and then stand upright again when we come to the line which begins לְפְנֵי. On the High Holy Days, the cantor or the reader while reciting these words falls face downward on the Bimah to show that the congregation is ready to accept the judgments of God, no matter what those judgments are.

THE KING OF KINGS
In the Aleinu we praise God,
Maker and Ruler of the universe.
We acknowledge His power, bow before Him,
and accept His judgments.

The Kaddish So the Adoration is a kind of summary of our whole service, though, of course, it is most important for what it says as we read it. But we could hardly complete our service without talking about the kind of world that we want so much, the kind of world we have called the End of Days. And, since it is a comfort to us to imagine how pleasant that time will be, this, too, is the prayer that we use in our service to comfort those who have lost a dear one through death.

We talked about this prayer earlier in the book, for it is special in another way, too: It is said in Aramaic and not in Hebrew. It was originally used at the funeral of scholars, but now we use it to remember all who died and who helped us in our search for a better life. The Kaddish is truly the best possible way for us to close our service, for it says that we should treasure our memory of those who have died by building the kind of world that they dreamed of.

Why Jews pray According to the tradition, one of the first prayers we say in the morning is Adon Olam and the last thing we do as we finish the prayers of Shaḥarit is to sing together Adon Olam. The Kotzker rabbi explained: We do this to show that the end of the service does not mean that we have given enough praise to God. No, it is better for us to see that we should start all over again each time that we come to the end. There is no end to the praise that we owe to God.

But our rabbis also taught us that prayer alone is not enough. A person must also behave according to the commandments. Otherwise, prayers become empty words, and we can not pray with true kavannah.

Another time, the Kotzker rabbi asked his students: "Do you know where to find the Lord?" And when they did not answer, he said: "The Lord is anywhere He is invited to enter."

When we Jews pray with all our hearts, with all our souls, and with all our might, we are asking God to come into our hearts. Of course, God is always with us, but we forget sometimes, and forgetting is like closing our minds to God. Prayer helps us to remember, it invites God to be with us, to come into our world, and to help us to know what is good.

The Prophet Micah taught us a wonderful lesson when he said, "It has been told you, O Man, what is good, and what the Lord, your God, asks of you: Only to do justly, to love mercy, and to walk humbly with your God." Prayer helps us to walk humbly with God, and so it leads us to do the right thing and to be kind to one another.

We Jews pray so that we can learn to act on our prayers.

PRAYING AND STRIVING
Striving to do right helps us pray
with kavannah. If we acknowledge God
as a God of mercy, we ourselves are merciful.
If we know Him as a God of justice,
we ourselves are fair.

no one is ever alone

So let me
Hear Your voice when I am ready.
Let me
Pause to sense You near;
And when I'm far away—
When peace seems but a distant dream—
I'll speak Your name and know
You are listening.

When trails seem to take me from You,
To valleys of darkness and shadow,
When all around, others are evil and unkind;
I will not fear, for You are with me.

I shall recall the days of light and glory,
Sun which shone on leaves of autumn hue;
Prayers my people spoke will lead me through:
"Surely goodness and mercy shall follow me all the days
    of my life;
And I shall dwell in the House of the Lord for ever."

O let me always remember
No one is separate;
No one is ever alone.

23

Talking it over

At times, praying is easy. The words seem to say just what you want to say, and you can feel that everything about your prayer is right. But sometimes, praying is just plain hard. Then, try as you will, you cannot get your mind to stay on the prayers. You might be worried about a fight that you had with a good friend. Or you may feel sick, your stomach all tied up inside or your head aching. Or you may feel so happy that you cannot keep your mind from wandering.

Sometimes the place is no help, either. We build our synagogues to be beautiful and inspiring; we fill them with symbols to remind us of God's laws and our people Israel. But sometimes we just don't feel like praying in the synagogue, no matter how nice it is. We feel instead like being outside in the cool air, or like walking in the mist, or like sitting comfortably at home.

Sometimes the people are no help. We pray with other people so that our prayers will not be selfish, so that we can come to know others well and learn to be good neighbors with them. We pray with other people so that we will know that our prayers are a part of the prayers of Jews everywhere.

But sometimes other people only disturb us. This one is too loud and that one never says anything. He is a bully and she is a nag. Other people can be annoying to us.

Even the prayers are no help at times. We use our prayerbook to help us pray together as a part of the Jewish people and of the congregation. We use the prayerbook because it is filled with the greatest hopes and prayers that we Jews have collected over the centuries. But sometimes the prayers seem strange; the words are not the words that we want to say. The prayers seem old and long. They get in our way. Somehow they keep us from praying.

What has happened? Can we know all that we have studied here and still not be able to pray? What are we supposed to do if we can't pray? Should we walk a bit by ourselves and try to pray in our own words? Or should we say that prayer just makes no sense and there is no reason to keep trying? Should we go to the synagogue and hate the prayers and the people? Or should we stop trying to pray and simply watch television?

Even the most religious people, people who pray every day, sometimes have trouble praying with kavannah. After all, a person is not a horse. **Prayer is personal**

If we teach a horse to turn pages, he'll keep on doing it as long as we remember to give him a few oats from time to time. But turning pages is not the same thing as praying.

Praying is very personal. No one can make you pray. You have to want to do it; you have to try. Sometimes it will come easy, and sometimes it will be very difficult. Sometimes it will be wonderful and make you feel really great. At other times you will feel terrible.

In a way, praying is like flying a kite. After all the thinking and the planning, after putting the kite together very carefully and making a nice long tail for it, and after running very hard to get it up in the air, it sometimes will not fly at all. Does that mean that you should stop trying? Not if you know how great it feels when your kite is soaring so high that it seems to touch the clouds passing by.

Of course, the more practice you get flying your kite, the better you get at flying it. And prayer is like that, too. The more practice you get praying, the more your prayers will seem to rise like a soaring kite.

PRACTICING PRAYER
Praying is sometimes easy, sometimes hard.
But we don't give up trying to pray
with kavannah. We keep on practicing prayer.

Praying regularly

It happened once that the watchmaker of a small village died. And, as there was no one else in the village who could repair watches, the townspeople did not know what to do when their clocks and watches stopped keeping time.

Some of the people, when their watches stopped, just threw the watches in the bottom of a drawer and left them there, piling other things on top of them and forgetting all about them. Other people, when their watches stopped, carefully wrapped and stored them, taking them out from time to time just to dust them off.

Now one day a new watchmaker came to town. Then all the people brought their broken watches to the new watchmaker. Now, as for the watches that had been carefully stored, the watchmaker had to make only a few minor adjustments and maybe put in a new part or two and those watches were as good as new. But, as for the watches that had been thrown aside, every part had to be cleaned and many parts had to be replaced before those watches would ever tick again.

The man who told this story, Abraham Joshua Heschel, went on to explain that it is this way with prayer, too. If we stop praying when our prayers don't seem to be working, and we don't bother to pray again until we feel like it, then we will have a very hard time starting to pray again. We will be like the people who did not bother to care for their watches. But if we are like the people who wrapped their watches carefully, and if we keep right on pray-

UNENDING PRAISE

Through unending prayer and praise
we Jews stay in prayer practice.
Our praying does not get "rusty"
like old watches, laid aside and forgotten.

ing even when we do not think that our prayer is doing any good, then when kavannah comes to us again, like the new watchmaker coming to town, we will be able to pray with all our hearts!

Only you can make prayer work for you. You have to practice praying. Day after day, you have to keep trying it until it becomes a part of your life. Then your days will seem special, brighter. And, even when you are not in the right mood, prayer will help you.

When you sit in your house

To bring prayer into our whole life, we must practice it at home, just as we do at the synagogue. We must give prayer the same kavannah when we are praying with our family as we do when we are praying with the congregation. If we do that, then prayer will help to make our home life special, too.

Judaism has given us many opportunities to pray at home. Every Friday evening, as we welcome the Shabbat, we can light the candles together with our family, say the blessing over wine, and over our Shabbat meal. And, as the Shabbat begins to depart, on the verge of beginning a new week, we can pray together the service of *Havdalah*, the Separation.

Havdalah separates the holy from the ordinary, the Shabbat from the rest of the week; it is a ceremony of great beauty. It is another of the wonderful customs which were given to us by the men of the Great Assembly, who gave us the berachah formula and the basic steps of the service.

And, of course, as the Holy Days come throughout the year, they bring new chances for us to pray at home with our family. At Ḥanukkah we pray together the berachah for lighting the candles. At Pesaḥ, we pray together the Seder service. At Sukkot, we can build together a sukkah and say together the blessing that reminds us of God's commandment about the sukkah.

But we don't have to wait for a special occasion. Every day is holy to God. Every meal is a chance to thank God for the kind of life we live, for our families and friends, and for the world around us. Each morning is a chance to thank God for the wonder of sleep, and for restoring us to the world. And every evening is a chance to speak the words of Shema even as we prepare to sleep, so that as we rest our thoughts may ever be of God.

You can see from the way we Jews have given a prayer for all things, that we must love prayer very dearly. And it is true, we do.

PRAYING AT HOME
In a Jewish home, we welcome the Shabbat with blessings. We bid it good-bye with the Havdalah. We pray together on Ḥanukkah, at Pesaḥ, and at Sukkot. We bless each meal, each evening, and each morning.

One reason that the Jewish people learned to love prayer so much was that prayer reminded us constantly of how we should live our lives day by day. When the rabbis told us to say one hundred berachot every day, they were really telling us to try to make every moment of our lives special by doing good things. Our prayers are not meant to take us out of this world and into the world of God. They are meant to bring God into our world.

The rabbis told this story to explain how our prayers should remind us of how to live justly:

A certain Jew, who happened to be a jeweler dealing in diamonds and pearls, was saying his evening prayers. As he was nearing the end of his devotions, another jeweler came rushing into the shop, looked for a moment at a pearl, and then said, "I want to buy this pearl. I will give you a hundred for it."

But, since the Jew was still praying, he could not answer the man. He had to concentrate all his mind on the prayers. And, since the Jew did not answer, the other jeweler said, "All right, if one hundred is not enough for this pearl, then I will give you two hundred for it."

Still the Jew did not answer. He was praying with kavannah and he refused to be disturbed by anything. Now the other jeweler raised his voice in anger and said, "All right, so you think that this pearl is so valuable that you will not even answer me. Tell me, will you sell it to me for three hundred?"

The Jew did not answer, for just then he was saying the silent prayer. "I will give you four hundred," said the impatient customer, "but that is my last offer."

Acting on prayer

Just then the Jew completed saying his prayers. He closed his prayerbook and looked into the eyes of the angry jeweler. "The pearl is yours for only one hundred."

Now the customer was amazed. "I offered you four hundred for this pearl. Why should you sell it to me for only a hundred?"

The Jew answered, "If you had come in when I was not praying, then I would have taken the first price of one hundred at once and sold you the pearl. Why should I cheat you now by taking more than I would normally? What good are all my prayers if I cannot act with honesty?"

The prayerful person

Our prayers remind us over and over of the kind of world we could have if we could all work together in peace. As we praise God for creating the world and the universe, we think of the gifts which we already have. And when we ask God to help us, we are asking for things which will help us to live better with one another. Praying often helps us to keep our mind on what our real job is in this world.

It does not matter if you become a scientist or a dentist, a lawyer or a doctor, an accountant or a construction worker, a policeman or a president. The real question that we Jews ask over and over is, "Will you be a good person?" Will you be a person who helps to bring peace and brightness into the world, a person who always acts to do the right thing even when it is very hard to do right, a person who stops to help others even when they are not friends but just people needing help? Will you be a person who helps to make the world brighter?

Our rabbis taught us that we should be like Moses' brother Aaron, who was the first High Priest of Israel. To show us why they chose Aaron as a good model for us to follow, they told this story:

Once Aaron learned that two men who had once been friends had quarreled and would not speak to one another. So Aaron went to one and he said, "Look, your friend has told me that he would like to apologize to you if you would just meet him in the field today."

Then Aaron went to the other man and said, "Your friend has told me that he would like to apologize to you. He is waiting for you there in the field."

When the two men met in the field, they embraced. They were both glad to make up. And they were both sorry they had quarreled.

The rabbis said that Aaron loved peace so much that he tried to make peace between men whenever he could. And this is the kind of person that our prayers teach us to be. The kind of a person who works always to bring peace and brotherhood into the world.

PRAYING AND DOING
Prayer reminds us to work for
a world of justice and goodwill.
That is why we Jews, like Aaron,
"seek peace and pursue it."

שָׁלוֹם The Hebrew word for peace, *Shalom*, contains the idea of fullness or completeness. And so, we end our book with a prayer. We pray to make our lives and the lives of all people complete by bringing peace to our world. And now that this book is complete, we thank God for helping us to complete it.

During the Middle Ages, it was a custom for Jews to end their books with thanks to God, the Author of life. And so the author of this book ends with the words of their prayer:

תַּם וְנִשְׁלָם.
שֶׁבַח לָאֵל.
בּוֹרֵא עוֹלָם:

Done and fulfilled,
Thanks to God,
Creator of the universe.

Amen.

Index to Prayers

PRAYERS FOUND IN HEBREW AND ENGLISH

אבינו מלכינו	Avinu Malkenu	168
אבות	Avot	143
אהבה רבה	Ahavah Rabbah	136
אין כאלהינו	En Kelohenu	12
אלהי. נצור	Elohai N'tzor	151
אשרי	Ashre	104
ברכו	Borchu	133
ברכת הכהנים	Birkat ha–Kohanim	157
ברכת המזון	Birkat ha–Mazon	46
ברכת התורה	Birkat ha–Torah	158
המוציא	Ha–Motzi	34
ואהבת	V'ahavta	138
ולירושלים	V'lirushalayim	147
יוצר אור	Yotzer Or	133
כל נדרי	Kol Nidre	169
מי־כמכה	Mi Chamocha	139
מודה אני	Modeh Ani	108
סלח לנו	Slaḥ Lanu	145
על חטא	Al Ḥet	171
עלינו	Aleinu	174
קדוש. קדוש. קדוש.	Kadosh, Kadosh, Kadosh	50
קדיש	Kaddish	105
שים שלום	Sim Shalom	149
שמע	Shema	137

BERACHOT GIVEN IN ENGLISH TRANSLATION

...Creator of the fruit of the trees.	48	...who give changing forms...	50
...Creator of the fruit of the vine.	48	...who have formed man	
...on the washing of the hands.	132	in wisdom...	95
...to affix the mezuzah.	97	...whose world lacks	
...who did not make me a slave.	94	nothing...	101

PRAYERS GIVEN IN ENGLISH VERSIONS

And you shall love . . .   75

Grant peace, welfare and blessing . . .   107

Grant us peace, Thy most precious gift . . .   107

Hear our voice . . .   144

I made pleasant songs . . .   78

If You had cattle . . .   101

It is a tree of life . . .   76

Lord our God, You have shown us
    great love . . .   26

The Lord upholds all who fall . . .   103

O You who hear weeping . . .   172

Please make the words of Your Torah . . .   132

Psalm 150   80

True it is . . .   139

You and I . . .   102

LIST OF LEGENDS AND STORIES

Daniel in the lions' den   8

The king's nightingale   15

The horse that prayed   23-26

Ḥayyim the Cantor   28-30

Prayer of the simple man   30-31

Thanks for bread   33-34

The most precious thing   37-39

The kidnaped prince   42-43

Voices of praise   52-53

The king's crown   67

Hot and cold wine   92-93

The spilled ink   121

The crazy dancers   127-128

The fox and the fish   156

The broken watches   182

The jeweler at prayer   185-186

Aaron the peacemaker   187

Index

Aaron, 157, 186-187
Abraham, 21, 62, 142-143
Adon Olam, 84, 176
Adonai Elohenu, 91-93, 98
Afikoman, 123
Aha, Rabbi, 66
Akiba, 62, 156
Al Het, 171
Alef Bet, 31, 103
Aleinu (Adoration), 161, 173-176
Am ha-Sefer, 155
Amen, 98-99
American Jews, 12, 85, 86, 160
Amidah, 68, 142, 144, 145, 148-149, 151, 161
Anim Zemirot, 78
Aramaic, 68-70, 104-106, 176
Aron Kodesh, 111, 113, 114, 115, 158, 172
Ashre, 103-104
Atah, 90-91
Avinu Malkenu, 168

Baal Koray (Master of Reading), 84
Baal Shem Tov, 86
Babylonia, 66, 70, 165
Bachya ibn Pakuda, Rabbi, 121
Baruch, 90
Berachot, 88-99, 131-135, 142-149, 153, 184, 185
Bet ha-Knesset, 110
Bet ha-Midrash, 110
Bet ha-Tefillah, 110-111
Bezalel, 114
Bible, 21-22, 30, 39, 53-55, 80, 83, 88-89, 91, 92, 97-99, 103, 117, 136, 137, 138
Bimah, 40, 114, 115, 175
Birkat ha-Mazon, 46, 47, 123
Birkot ha-Shahar, 131, 132-133
Borchu, 66, 68, 84, 104-105, 133, 166

Cantors, 28-30, 82-83, 169
Commandments, 14, 26, 77, 96, 113, 138-139, 147, 153, 155, 157, 162, 184
Conservative Jews, 66, 81, 86
Covenant, 71, 164, 167

Dancing, 40-41, 127-128, 153, 162-163
Daniel, 8, 89
David, King, 80, 147
Deuteronomy, 98
Dona Dona, 85

Egypt, 124, 125, 130, 139, 140, 167
Eleazar, Rabbi, 35

Eliezer, Rabbi, 43
Elohim, 91
En Kelohenu, 12, 67
End of Days, 61, 176
English, 74, 85, 91, 108
Esther, Book of, 88-89
Etz Hayyim, 115

Festivals, 84, 88, 162, 164-165, 173
Forgiveness, see Sin and forgiveness
Four Questions, 46, 123
Friends (Quakers), 71-72

Great Assembly, 88-89, 184

Haftarah, 83, 87
Haggadah, 122-126
Hallel service, 130-131
Ha-Motzi, 46, 48
Hanukkah, 96, 114, 119, 184
Hanukkiah, 114
Hasidim, 15, 30, 40-41, 86, 153
Havdalah (the Separation), 183, 184
Hayyim the Cantor, 28-30
Hebrew, 36, 68, 70, 74, 76, 83, 90-91, 98-99, 104, 110, 113, 138, 188
Herzl, Theodor, 51
Heschel, Abraham Joshua, 182
Hillel, 42
Holy Ark, 111, 113; see also Aron Kodesh
Holy Days, 45, 83, 84, 130, 149, 164-171, 184
Hoshen, 116

Ibn Ezra, 79
Isaac, 62, 142
Israel (people), 26, 66, 79, 112, 114, 116, 139, 140-141, 144, 146, 165
Israel, State of, 12, 79, 114, 147, 148
Israelis, 85, 114

Jacob, 62, 142, 143
Jerusalem, 40, 88, 117, 147, 172
Judah Ha-Hasid, 43
Judah the Prince, Rabbi, 49
Judaism, 42, 51, 54, 104, 126, 154, 170
Justice and mercy, 9, 71, 92-93, 108, 117, 137, 168, 177, 187

Kaddish, 70, 104-106, 176
Kavannah, 26, 28-31, 68, 71, 72, 81, 84, 86, 87, 100, 111, 117, 121, 129, 152, 159, 160, 177, 181, 183, 185
Keter, 115, 116
Kiddush, 84
Kohanim, 82
Kol Nidre, 70, 79, 84, 169-170

Kook, Rav, 154
Kotzker Rabbi, the, 176, 177

Laws, 27, 60, 77, 116, 121, 122, 124, 138,
    158-159, 164, 168, 179
Lechah Dodi, 82
Levites, 80
Love and lovingkindness, 13-15, 27, 28, 42, 46,
    47, 49, 51, 58, 71, 103, 116, 117, 136-138, 167
Luhot ha-Berit, 113

Ma'ariv, 129
Mahzor, 165
Mar, Rabbi, 151, 152
Medzibozer rebbe, 39
Melech ha-Olam, 93
Menorah, 113, 114
Mercy, see Justice and Mercy
Messiah, 14, 118, 144
Mezuzah, 97, 155, 162
Mi Chamocha, 136
Midrash, stories from, 52-53, 92-93, 101
Minhah service, 129, 131, 171
Minyan, 65-67, 133
Miriam, 40, 81
Mishnah, 68, 132, 155
Mitzvot, 96-99, 118, 159
Modeh Ani, 108
Modim, 64, 101, 161
Moses, 40, 62, 67, 113, 157, 186
Mount Moriah, 148
Mount Sinai, 113
Musaf, 130, 165, 166
Music, 78, 87; see also Singing

Neilah service, 171-172
Ner Tamid, 114
Nigun, 86
Nusah, 84, 87

Oneness of God, 21-22, 42, 50, 64, 101, 137, 141,
    174-175
Oriental Jews, 86
Orthodox Jews, 86

Palestine, 70
Peace, 9, 21, 22, 43, 51, 62, 65, 71, 99, 106, 107,
    118, 137, 148, 187, 188
People of the Book, 155-156
Pesah, 45, 46, 120, 122-126, 184
Poetry, 74-77, 78, 164
Prayerbook, 53, 55, 59, 68, 76, 87, 100, 107-108, 120,
    151, 165, 180
Prayer-games, 102-104
Priestly Blessing, 157
Prophets, 51, 83, 88, 177
Psalms, 39, 57, 80, 81, 103, 130-131, 133, 152, 164,
    167

Rabbis, 15, 30, 31, 36, 39, 43, 53, 65, 99, 102, 115,
    121, 129, 131, 141, 144, 151, 154-155, 159, 176-177,
    185, 186, 187
Red Sea, 40, 79
Reform Jews, 66, 81, 86, 104, 132-133
Return, the, 147, 148
Rimmon, 116
Romans, 81, 155-156
Rosh Hashanah, 167, 168, 173-174

Samuel, Books of, 80
Saul (King), 80
Secunda, Sholom, 85
Seder, Pesah, 46, 120-126, 184
Sefer Torah, 115, 165, 166
Sephardic synagogues, 114-115
Shabbat (Sabbath), 10, 81, 82, 85, 96, 114, 130, 149,
    162, 165, 166, 183-184
Shaharit service, 129, 130, 131
Shalom, 188
Shalom Alechem, 85
Sheliah Tsibur, 82, 83, 84
Shema, 8, 26, 39, 64, 67, 68, 97, 128, 129, 136, 137,
    140-141, 155, 160-162, 174
Shofar, 167, 172
Sholom Secunda, 85
Siddur, 120, 154
Sim Shalom, 84
Simha Bunam, Rabbi, 43
Simhat Torah, 40, 165, 166
Sin and forgiveness, 36-39, 42, 55, 136, 143-146, 167,
    170-172
Singing, 15, 28-30, 40, 53, 78-87, 153
Specialness (quality of), 10, 45-51, 74, 79, 97, 99,
    101, 108, 111, 164, 167, 185
Study, 10-11, 27, 39, 110, 112, 115, 119, 125, 132,
    134-135, 137, 145, 154-159
Sukkot, 184
Symbols, 76-77, 112-117, 169
Synagogues, 12, 17, 30, 40, 81, 82, 89, 94, 109-117,
    152, 169, 179

Tallit, 150, 162
Talmud, 58, 66, 70, 82, 109, 110, 151, 157, 166
Tefillah, 142-149, 161, 162, 167
Temple, 80-83, 114, 115, 117, 128, 129, 148, 157,
    166
Torah, 26-29, 39, 40, 66, 68, 76-77, 111, 113, 115,
    116, 130, 132, 137, 138, 154-159, 165
Trop, 83, 84
Tsitsit, 162

Yad, 116
Yiddish, 85, 110, 160
Yitzhak, Rabbi, 66
Yom Kippur, 70, 79, 167-172